LVF
TEL

ɔ
t alr
ɔ, by v
ie

8

Gallery Books
Editor: Peter Fallon

CONVERSATIONS ON A
HOMECOMING

By the same author

Thomas Murphy

CONVERSATIONS ON A HOMECOMING

Gallery Books

Conversations on a Homecoming
is first published
simultaneously in paperback
and in a clothbound edition
on 16 September 1986.

The Gallery Press
19 Oakdown Road
Dublin 14, Ireland.

© Thomas Murphy 1986

ISBN 0 904011 94 1 (*paperback*)
0 904011 95 X (*clothbound*)

All performing rights in the play are strictly reserved. Applica-
tions for amateur productions must be made in advance to The
Gallery Press and for professional productions to Frazer &
Dunlop Ltd., 91 Regent Street, London WIR 8RU or Ms. B.
Aschenberg, ICM, 40 West 57th Street, N.Y., N.Y. 10019.
The Gallery Press receives financial assistance from The Arts
Council/An Chomhairle Ealaíon, Ireland.

Conversations on a Homecoming was first performed by the
Druid Theatre Company, Galway, on 16 April 1985, with
the following cast:

TOM	Sean McGinley
MICHAEL	Paul Brennan
JUNIOR	Macliosa Stafford
LIAM	Ray McBride
PEGGY	Marie Mullen
MISSUS	Pat Leavy
ANNE	Jane Brennan

Direction	Garry Hynes
Design	Frank Conway
Lighting	Barbara Bradshaw

Time and place
The early 1970s. A pub in a town in east Galway.

To the cast, director and designers
and to all Galway Druids
past, present and future

Conversations
on a Homecoming

A run-down pub. Outside, the faded signboard reads THE WHITE
HOUSE; *inside similarly. The place is in need of decoration, the stock
on the shelves is sparse, a clock on a wall permanently reading ten
past four, a dusty picture of John F. Kennedy . . . . The only thing that
appears to be new is a cheap partition which has been erected to divide
the room into two, a Public Bar (not seen) and the Lounge which is
the main acting area.*

The lights come up on ANNE. *She is seventeen, standing behind the
counter, motionless, staring blankly out the window, her expression
simple and grave. A tapping on the counter in the public bar; it is
repeated before she reacts and moves off to serve a customer.*

TOM *is hunched in his overcoat, seated at a table, sipping from a
half-pint glass of Guinness, reading a newspaper: his feet resting on
the rung of another chair give him a posture that is almost foetal. He
is in his late thirties.*

JUNIOR *is entering front door and hallway. He pauses in door to
investigate momentarily the sound of a car pulling into the car park.*
JUNIOR *is thirty-one, more casually dressed than the others (a duffel
coat and a good heavy pullover), a contented, unaffected man; a big
— though simple — sense of humour; an enviable capacity to enjoy
himself. En route to the counter:*

JUNIOR Well, bolix!
TOM (*Mildly*) Oh? (*And continues with his newspaper*)
JUNIOR (*At the counter, poking his head around the end of the
partition*) Well, Anne! How yeh, Johnny! (*Exaggerated
nasal brogue*) We'll have Ihrost!

Chuckle, off, in reaction: We will, a dhiabhail . . . .

9

JUNIOR (*To* TOM) He didn't come in yet?

TOM Was that him?

JUNIOR No. What are you having, boy?

TOM Pint.

JUNIOR Two pints, Anne. (*To* TOM) Liam Brady pulling into the car park. Well, Anne! Are you well?

ANNE (*Almost silently; smiles*) Fine.

> LIAM *entering, car keys swinging, about the same age as* JUNIOR; *well-dressed and groomed: expensive, heavy pinstripe, double-breasted suit, a newspaper neatly folded sticking out of his pocket for effect. He is a farmer, an estate agent, a travel agent, he owns property . . . . he affects a slight American accent; a bit stupid and insensitive — seemingly the requisites of success.*

LIAM Hi! (TOM *merely glances up*) Hi, Junie!

JUNIOR How yeh.

LIAM What's bringing ye in here?

JUNIOR Michael Ridge is home from America.

LIAM Hi, Anne! (*Craning over the bar to see if there is anyone in the public bar*)

JUNIOR We'll get all the news. What are you having?

LIAM (*Indecisive*) Ahm . . . .

JUNIOR It's all the same to me.

LIAM Had me a few shots earlier. Pint.

JUNIOR Three pints, Anne.

> LIAM *joins* TOM, *takes out his newspaper, is not interested in it, is replacing/arranging it in his pocket again.*

TOM Give us a look at that (*the newspaper*). What time is it?

LIAM It's nearly eight.

TOM (*Disinterestedly*) And what has you in here?

LIAM Oh.

JUNIOR Thanks, Anne. (*Takes first pint to table*) There's only Johnny Quinn in the public bar.

Off, the town clock chiming eight.

LIAM That town clock is fast.

JUNIOR He was taking his mother or something out the country to see relations. I lent him the car.

TOM I thought he might be here sooner.

JUNIOR No. He said he'd hardly make it before eight. A reunion, wuw! We'll get all the news.

LIAM He didn't bring a bus home with him then?

JUNIOR No — Thanks, Anne — I lent him the car. (*Taking the other two pints to the table quietly*) He was anxious to see JJ too.

LIAM JJ was up in Daly's earlier. On another batter. Getting mighty opstreperous, fellas, mighty maudlin.

TOM (*To himself*) Are they singing up in Daly's? The cowboys.

JUNIOR (*Suddenly*) I'm not staying out late tonight.

TOM What? (*Chucks Liam's paper aside*) And who's asking yeh?

They have been waiting for their pints to 'settle'. Off, the church clock is chiming eight.

LIAM (*A minor triumph for his watch*) There, the church clock, eight!

TOM Another discrepancy between Church and State.

LIAM What?

TOM Nothing. Good luck!

JUNIOR Luck, boy!

LIAM Good luck, fellas!

JUNIOR (*Appreciative gasp after a long draught*) Aaa, Jasus! (*And starts to sing absently to himself*) 'They were only a bunch of violets, violets so blue / Fresh and fair and dainty, they sparkled like the dew / Fresh and fair and dainty, they sparkled like the dew / But I'll not forget old Ireland far from the old folks at home.'

During this, MISSUS has come down the stairs (which are at the end of the hall), gone into the public bar — a greeting, off, to Johnny — and now reappears behind

11

the counter in the lounge. She is in her early fifties, carelessly dressed (a dirty house-coat); a worried, slow-moving drudge of a woman, senses a bit numbed by life, but trying to keep the place together.

MISSUS   Aa, the boys.
JUNIOR   Hello, Missus! (*And continues another jumbled verse of the song to himself*) .
MISSUS   Yas.
LIAM   How do, Mrs. Kilkelly!
MISSUS   And Liam.

She whispers something to ANNE *and* ANNE *goes about collecting her coat to go on some errand.*

LIAM   The partition is holding up well?
MISSUS   Yas. Thanks. Yas, Liam (*Smiles/drools at* LIAM, *and she exits to public bar*) Cold enough, Johnny?
JUNIOR   (*To himself*) We'll have fhrost.
TOM   Shh!

TOM *has been listening to a car pulling into the car park.* ANNE *is pulling on her overcoat going out front door when she bumps into* MICHAEL *who is entering.*

MICHAEL   Oops!
ANNE   Sorry.
MICHAEL   Sorry.

A backward glance from ANNE *at him as she exits.* MICHAEL *pauses for a brief moment to muster himself before going into the lounge. He is the same age as* TOM; *defensively inclined towards the supercilious, false panache to hide his failure.*

MICHAEL   Hello there!
JUNIOR   Hah, here he is!
TOM   Oh, look in!
LIAM   The man himself!
MICHAEL   Gee! Gee! Lot of changes round here!

TOM   Don't start that game now — How yeh, you're welcome,
      how yeh!
LIAM (*Pushing awkwardly through them, nearly spilling
      Junior's pint*) Well, howdy, Mick!
JUNIOR (*Protecting his pint*) Jasus, the cowboy! (*Liam*)
MICHAEL Liam! And how are you?
LIAM Good to see yeh, well good to see yeh!
TOM   That's a fancy-lookin' suit you have on.
MICHAEL What's fancy about it?
TOM   Nothing.
LIAM You look just great!
TOM   (*Shaking hands*) Well? How yeh, you're welcome, how
      yeh?
MICHAEL Not too bad.
JUNIOR Not three bad, what're you having, boy?
TOM   Oh, a brandy, a brandy, a brandy for the emigrant, don't
      yeh know well?
LIAM Pull up a pew, fella.
MICHAEL I'll have a pint, Junie.
JUNIOR Fair play to yeh. (*Going to counter*) Missus!
TOM   Well?
MICHAEL How are you?
TOM   I'm alright.
JUNIOR (*Impatient at counter*) Missus!
TOM   You're lookin' well.
MICHAEL Can't help it. You know?
TOM   I suppose you can't.
JUNIOR (*To* MISSUS *who has entered behind counter*) A pint,
      please.
LIAM A holiday, Mick?
MICHAEL Ah . . . yeh. (LIAM *nods in that solemn provincial way,
      eyes fixed on* MICHAEL *in ignorant assessment*) And how
      are things with you, Liam?
LIAM Fightin' fit, fella.
MICHAEL The farming, the rates collecting, the —
TOM   Oh and sure he's an auctioneer too now.
MICHAEL Yeh?
LIAM Estate agent, Mick.
TOM   Took out his diploma after intensive and in-depth study
      last year.

13

JUNIOR (*From counter*) M.I.5.A.A.!

MICHAEL What?

TOM Junior's sense of humour.

LIAM M.I.A.A., Mick.

JUNIOR Letters after his name and the car he drives doesn't need a clutch!

MICHAEL So business is good then?

LIAM Property-wise, this country, A-one, Mick. This country, Mick, last refuge in Europe.

MICHAEL Good begod, I came to the right place then.

JUNIOR Thanks, Missus. (*He is waiting for his change*)

TOM You haven't much of an accent.

MICHAEL (*British accent*) Only for the stage.

TOM (*British accent*) Yes, yes, good show, jolly good, right chaps, it's up to us, we're going through: John Mills.

MICHAEL Aw, he's making better ones now.

TOM Is he?

JUNIOR Thanks, Missus.

MISSUS (*Retreating off, fingering her dirty house-coat*) Aa, Michael.

We see her a few moments later reappear from the public bar into the hallway and going upstairs.

MICHAEL How's your mother, Tom?

TOM Oh, she's fine.

MICHAEL And the school?

TOM Fine. The headmaster might drop dead any day now —

JUNIOR (*Setting pint in front of* MICHAEL) Now, boy —

TOM And my subsequent rise in station and salary will make all the difference.

MICHAEL Thanks, Junie.

TOM What brought you back?

MICHAEL Oh, before I forget them — (*He gives car keys to* JUNIOR) Thanks.

JUNIOR Not at all, boy.

TOM Hmm? At this time of the year.

JUNIOR Jasus, you weren't home for . . .

TOM Must be ten years.

JUNIOR That race week. (*He starts to laugh*)

TOM Aw Jay, that Galway race week!

They start to laugh.

JUNIOR Aw Jasus, d'yeh remember your man?
TOM Aw God, yes, your man!
JUNIOR Aw Jasus, Jasus! (*Junior's laugh usually incorporates 'Jasus'*)
TOM The cut of him!
JUNIOR Aw Jasus, Jasus!
LIAM Who?
JUNIOR D'yeh remember?
MICHAEL I do.
JUNIOR But do yeh? — Jasus, Jasus!
LIAM Who was this?
JUNIOR Do yeh, do yeh, remember him?
MICHAEL (*Laughing*) I do, I do!
JUNIOR Jasus, Jasus!

Junior's laugh is infectious, all laughing. Ritual toast again.

MICHAEL Good luck, Junie!
JUNIOR Good luck phatever (*whatever*)!
TOM Good luck!
LIAM Good luck, fellas!

They drink.

MICHAEL Is JJ around?
TOM No. But what brought you back? (MICHAEL *glances at him, unsure*) So sudden. This time of the year.
JUNIOR Nos-taigia.
MICHAEL Something like that.
TOM What?
MICHAEL (*Forces a laugh*) The White House, our refuge, our wellsprings of hope and aspiration. (*Mimicking JJ/ Kennedy*) Let the word go forth from this time and place to friend and foe alike that the torch has been passed to a new generation!

15

LIAM JJ doing his Kennedy bit, is it? Making speeches. (*Dismissive*) JJ.
MICHAEL (*To* LIAM) We virtually built this place with JJ. Right, Tom?
JUNIOR Jasus we did.
MICHAEL Night after night, while you were wasting all those years away at university.
JUNIOR Jasus we did. And pints.
TOM (*To* JUNIOR) Sure you were only a boy.
MICHAEL You wrote your rightest poems here.
TOM (*Laughing at himself*) I did — and read them!
MICHAEL You wrote that speech — JJ's inaugural — for our opening (*JJ/Kennedy voice again*) Friends, all this, our cultural centre has been a co-sponsorial job from design to décor. Mark its line, its adornment —
TOM I never said 'mark' —
MICHAEL Its atmosphere derives from no attribute of wild wisdom, vestige of native cunning, or selfish motive. The day of the dinosaur is gone forever. And with it the troglodytian attitude incarcerated in the cave whence it came.
TOM Troglodytical.
MICHAEL And as I look around me, I know that some of us will be departing —
JUNIOR To ride the waves or drown in them.
MICHAEL That's it, Junie —
JUNIOR (*Pleased with himself*) As the fella says —
MICHAEL To seek the new ideas. And some of us will remain, custodians of this, *our* White House, to keep the metaphorical doors of thought, hope, generosity, expression, aspiration open. So that all will find — the denizen of this hamlet, the traveller in his frequent returnings — a place of fulfilment, or a refuge if need be. Something like that. You wrote that.
TOM (*Chuckling*) I suppose I did. Sure we'd all have been departing, riding the waves, if we paid heed to poor auld JJ. (LIAM *laughs*) But you didn't tell us: What brought you back?
MICHAEL I told you. Lost horizons.
TOM Wha! (*First wonderings: Can he be serious*)

16

MICHAEL No.

TOM What?

MICHAEL No, you'd be surprised at how dicked-up one can get — I mean, how meaningless things can become for one — occasionally of course — away from one's — you know.

TOM I suppose 'one' can. (*Awkward moment's pause*) But you're looking well.

MICHAEL Can't help it.

LIAM (*Eyes all the time fastened on* MICHAEL) It could be a good stand for a fella, Mick? This place, properly handled.

MICHAEL (*Joking*) You didn't consider taking up the gun and marching on the North?

JUNIOR We thought about it. (MICHAEL *laughs*) Serious.

MICHAEL What?

JUNIOR We did.

LIAM We nearly did.

JUNIOR Serious.

LIAM Shoot us a few Prods.

MICHAEL *looks at* TOM.

TOM It's very bad up there.

MICHAEL I know, I've been reading, but.

LIAM We nearly did, one night.

TOM The way the Catholics are being treated.

MICHAEL (*Trying to conceal his disbelief*) Yeh?

LIAM A geezer up there in the papers one evening talking about coming down here and burning us all to the ground.

JUNIOR We know where to lay our hands on a few guns.

LIAM Well, I'm telling you, when I read that.

MICHAEL Guns!

JUNIOR We did. *He* (*Tom*) did.

MICHAEL (*Laughs in disbelief*) You did, Tom?

TOM (*Frowning*) What?

LIAM (*Boasting*) I was awful drunk that night, I was awful sick — Did ye see me?

MICHAEL (*Because* TOM *is still frowning*) No, I believe — I believe things are pretty bad alright, but, a baby and all now, Junie?

17

JUNIOR Oh-oh.
MICHAEL And how is Peggy, Tom?
TOM Fine.
MICHAEL Yeh? She's okay?
TOM Fine. I sent her word we'd be in here.
MICHAEL Any signs of yeh doing it yet — as the saying goes?
TOM Aren't we engaged, isn't that enough?
JUNIOR Jasus, ten years engaged!
TOM (*Mock belligerence*) Well, isn't it better than nothing!
JUNIOR (*Laughing*) Aw Jasus, Jasus!
LIAM But he's bought the site, Mick.
TOM And isn't it doubled in value now!
LIAM Trebled, trebled, fella!
JUNIOR Jasus, ten years engaged!
TOM D'yeh hear Sonny?
JUNIOR Jasus, Jasus!
TOM Napkin-head, procreation hope!
JUNIOR What does that mean, sir?
TOM Dick!

> *They laugh.*
> *During this last,* MISSUS *has come down the stairs, along hallway and is entering lounge, now minus her dirty house-coat, wearing her best cardigan.*

MISSUS Aa, the boys. And Liam. You're welcome, Michael.
MICHAEL Hello, Missus.
MISSUS Welcome, yas, now.
MICHAEL You're looking well.
MISSUS Oh now, pulling the divil by the tail. Isn't that the way, boys? But your mother is delighted, yas, the surprise of your visit. I was talking to her for a minute this morning in the post office and she was telling me. Now.
MICHAEL We were just saying we had some great times here, what?
MISSUS Yas, but Liam is the boy that's doing well. Waiting for the right girl. And poor Tom waiting on you there this hour.
TOM I am indeed, Missus, the hound.
MISSUS Aa, sure he doesn't mean that at all. Usen't we call the two of you the twins one time. Always together, always

together. D'ye know now. Yas.

JUNIOR (*Quietly*) Yas, the twins.

MISSUS Yas, the twins. Aa I think Junior is a bit of a rogue.

TOM A blackguard, Missus.

MISSUS Aa, no joking. D'ye know now. A nice wife and a baby and a home of his own to go into. The way everyone should be.

JUNIOR (*To* TOM) Now.

MISSUS Isn't that right, Liam?

LIAM That is c'rrect, Mrs. Kilkelly.

MISSUS A nice sensible girl, and not be roaming the world.

JUNIOR (*To* MICHAEL) Now.

MICHAEL How is JJ?

MISSUS Oh JJ is — very well, thank you.

MICHAEL The time of our lives putting this place together, we were just saying. Do you remember the night — Where's the painting of the nude?

MISSUS Yas, but you're doing well, your mother was saying and are you alright there now, boys?

JUNIOR Well, you might start filling another round. (*To* TOM) Your round.

MISSUS Certainly. (*Going back to the bar*) Nice to see you all again.

JUNIOR She's desperate slow on the aul' pints.

MICHAEL *is still looking after her, shaken by the transformation that has come over her.*

MICHAEL She was the first lady. But where is JJ?

TOM Sure the man is dyin'.

MICHAEL What!

TOM Drinkin' himself to death, don't be talking.

LIAM That's where she sent the young one, out looking for him.

MICHAEL Did you tell him I'd be here? (JUNIOR *nods*) And?

JUNIOR He isn't together at all: he's on a batter.

MICHAEL But you told him?

JUNIOR *nods.*

LIAM He's probably gone into Galway or some place by now.
MICHAEL But he'll show up?
TOM You won't see him for a week. What about yourself?
LIAM (*Pleasure of the anticipation on his face*) I'll have the selling of this place before long.
TOM What about yourself?
MICHAEL What?
LIAM Gals.
JUNIOR 'Gals'. Jasus, you have more of an American accent than him!
TOM There was a rumour some time back you were married.
MICHAEL No.
TOM What?
MICHAEL Free love.
TOM Oh God!
MICHAEL Who was the bird I bumped into at the door?
JUNIOR Fair play to yeh!
MICHAEL A young one.
LIAM You never lost it, Mickeen!
MICHAEL As a matter of fact I did. Plenty of it, too much of it over there.
TOM What about our new bank clerk for him, Junie.
JUNIOR Grrrrrah, Josephine!
TOM We have a right one for yeh.
LIAM (*To himself*) Dirty aul' thing.
JUNIOR She stays here and all: a quick nip up the stairs on your way out tonight and 'wham, bang, alikazam!'
TOM The most ridiculous whore of all times.
JUNIOR No bra.
LIAM Dirty aul' thing.
MICHAEL Why so ridiculous?
TOM A bank clerk, a bank clerk! A girl in her position!
JUNIOR (*Whispering*) And they say she wears no knickers either. Ich bin ein Berliner!
TOM (*Frowning*) What were you going to say?
MICHAEL No, but this young one at the door, that wasn't her.
LIAM Who?
MICHAEL A blue coat, fair, about eighteen.
JUNIOR Anne. (*It doesn't register with* MICHAEL)
TOM Anne, Annette.

JUNIOR Missus's daughter —
TOM JJ's daughter.
MICHAEL (*Brightening*) Well-well!
JUNIOR She's turning out nice on me word?
MICHAEL Annette. JJ's daughter. I bumped into her at the door
and I got the whiff of soap, sort of schoolgirl kind of
soap.
TOM It took you back?
MICHAEL It did.
TOM Tck!
MICHAEL No, there's a distinctive kind of aroma off —
TOM Gee, aroma. It'd be great to be young again.
MICHAEL You're a bogman, Ryan.
TOM I've no sensitivity alright.

> *They are chuckling.* JUNIOR *draining his glass as*
> MISSUS *arrives with one pint which she puts before*
> LIAM.

MISSUS Now, Liam. The other three are coming, boys. (*Returning to bar*)
MICHAEL Well, news!

> *Short pause; all thinking.*

JUNIOR Molloy's dog got killed by a tractor last month.
TOM Did you hear Stephen Riley died?
MICHAEL No! (TOM *nods*) Hoppy?
TOM Yeh, with the limp.
MICHAEL Well did he?
TOM He did.
JUNIOR D'yeh remember the Christmas he split the wife with the
crucifix? (*They laugh. Solemnly*) The Lord have mercy
on him.

> *He waits to meet their eyes and they burst into irreve-*
> *rent laughter.*

TOM And of course you know Larry, Larry O'Kelly got transferred?

MICHAEL Yeh. I was looking around for his painting of the nude.

JUNIOR Transferred, and *'Bridget Reclining'* with him.

MICHAEL It used to hang there.

TOM JJ defying Church and State hanging a nude.

JUNIOR And the priest, Father Connolly — Benny Diction — remember the grand accent he had? Jasus! — was up and down here, hotfoot about the nude.

TOM That wasn't why —

JUNIOR (*Taking fresh pint that was set before* LIAM) Here, cowboy, gimme that pint and I'll be working away on it.

MICHAEL And JJ: 'I do not speak for the Church on public matters, Father, and the Church is not going to speak for me'!

JUNIOR Good luck!

MICHAEL And JJ sent Benny Diction packing.

TOM He didn't.

MICHAEL He did.

JUNIOR (*After appreciative draught*) Aaa, Jasus!

MICHAEL 'When long-held power leads men towards arrogance, art reminds them of their limitations'!

JUNIOR Father Connolly called it a dirty picture.

TOM ⎱ He didn't!
MICHAEL ⎰ 'When long-held power narrows men's minds, art, poetry, music cleanses — '

TOM He called it a *bad* picture —

MICHAEL As far as you're concerned then, Father —

JUNIOR ⎱ 'Art galleries — '
MICHAEL ⎰ 'Art galleries — '

Michael and Junior laugh.

MICHAEL 'As far as you are concerned then, Father, art galleries all over the world are filled with dirty pictures?'

TOM (*Playing Fr. Connolly*) 'Please, please — Boys! — please don't talk to me about art galleries. Holy Moses, I've visited hundreds of them. You see, boys, I am a man who has travelled the world — '

MICHAEL 'I heard you spent a few years in Nigeria, but remember you're not talking to the Blacks now!'

Junior collects the other three pints, paying MISSUS.

MISSUS ⎱ Now, boys, yas.
JUNIOR ⎰ 'You're not talking to the Blacks now.'
TOM Aw but do ye see? The arrogance and condescension which you impute to Fr. Connolly's remarks were only too evident in our swinging liberal JJ's statements.
MICHAEL What does that mean?
JUNIOR That's what I was going to say.

Tom waives the question.

LIAM Good luck, fellas!
TOM The reason, the *real* reason, behind Father Connolly's visits had nothing to do with the painting.
MICHAEL He wanted JJ to take it down.
TOM That was the *ostensible* reason. The real reason was to tell JJ to behave himself like a good boy, to *warn* him.
JUNIOR And JJ *didn't* take it down — fair play to him.
MICHAEL To *warn* him?
TOM A token glance at the nude, a few token remarks about art galleries or something, and 'Haw haw-haw, you are a son-of-a-bachelor, John-John'. The real reason. 'You see, John-John, pub, club, art-centre, whatever it is you are running here, people are growing concerned. And particularly since your trade to date seems to be in the young. Already there have been complaints, indeed visits to the presbytery from worried parents and other concerned parties.'
JUNIOR The opposition, Paddy Joe Daly, and the other wise publicans.
TOM 'One native son, a guileless youth it appears, is about to leave a respectable clerkship which I had a hand in getting him myself — '
MICHAEL He never spoke for me!
TOM 'And a widowed mother — '
MICHAEL My mother never went near —
TOM 'To go off to Dublin to become — of all things! — an actor.'
MICHAEL Maybe your mother did.
TOM 'While another is suddenly contemplating leaving a

23

secure pensionable position. Think of it! A teacher! The first from the generations of plebs to which he belongs to make such breakthrough — to the professions! And going off without prospects, John-John, to God knows where!'

JUNIOR To become a writer.

TOM 'Others. Youths!'

JUNIOR Taking to hard liquor — Wuw!

TOM 'And all, it would appear, being influenced by something called the *vision* of a Johnny-come-lately.'

LIAM That's right, fellas. JJ was a blow-in, a cute buff-sham from back there Caherlistrane-side.

TOM 'Too far too fast for us, John-John.'

MICHAEL And that was the warning?

TOM (*Silent 'No'*) 'I think — John — you would be well advised to leave the decision-making to the parents and their spiritual advisors as to what is best for their children. I know you have it in you to take careful account of what I have said and the *security* of wiser steps.'

MICHAEL That sounds more like a threat.

TOM 'Holy Moses, Michael — John-John — we don't threaten anyone. We don't have to. We, the poor conservatives — troglodytes, if you will — have seen these little phases come and go. All we have to do is wait.'

MICHAEL *laughs. Then ritual toast:*

MICHAEL Good luck!

TOM 'God bless you.'

JUNIOR Luck!

LIAM Good luck, fellas!

MICHAEL But he might show up. (TOM *shakes his head*) Aw, you'd never know.

TOM *throws his head back at* MICHAEL'S *romantic hope springing eternal.*

LIAM Strangers wanting to run the town.

MICHAEL There was never anything like it before. And where did

24

that lousy partition come out of?

> TOM *and* JUNIOR — *with no great interest* — *notice the partition for the first time.*

LIAM   No decent heating in the place. The place was mighty cold without that.

MICHAEL   And how is Silver Strand?

LIAM   Oh! Oh!

JUNIOR   Tell him.

LIAM   Aw no, fellas!

JUNIOR   Tell him! The place is crawling with priests and police since the bishop's niece got poled back there last year — Tell him.

LIAM   Well. Well, I shifted this Judy at a dance in Seapoint and wheeled her back to the Strand, and we were coorting away there nicely — No! No! A fair coort mind! I hadn't even bothered to let back the seats of the auld jalop. But next thing — suddenly — my heart was in my mouth. Tap-tap-tap at the window, and it all fogged up. A big policeman with a flashlamp. What are yeh doin' there, says he. Kneckin', fella, says I. Well, says he — Well, says he, stick your neck now back in your trousers and hump off.

> *They laugh.*

JUNIOR   Tell him about Dooley.

TOM   Aw wait'll I tell yeh.

JUNIOR   Yeh remember Dooley?

MICHAEL   The librarian is it?

TOM   Shiny boots —

JUNIOR   Holy Harry —

TOM   First Mass, Communion, a pillar of the community. Well, it's all an act. He hates it all: Church, State, every-thing.

JUNIOR   Jasus, Jasus, Jasus . . . .

TOM   Stall it a minute now. The headmaster sent me down to organise some kind of library service with him for the school and we got talking. And d'yeh know his great secret rebellion against it all? Called me down to the shelf like this. *The Life Story of the Little Flower* filed under horticulture. Well laugh when I saw it? I nearly died. And giggling away to himself. The malice! I never enjoyed anything so much. (*Laughter subsiding*) Well yourself?

MICHAEL Oh, having a great time. You know?

TOM *News! News!*

MICHAEL Well, I was with this buddy of mine one night and we picked up these two chicks in a bar.

LIAM Yeh? —

JUNIOR Yeh?

MICHAEL Well. It was coming to closing time anyway and they're clearing the glasses away, see, and one of the barmen — just like that — grabbed the glass out of one of the chick's hands —

LIAM Yeh? —

JUNIOR Yeh?

MICHAEL And this buddy of mine — he's only a little guy — took a swing at the barman, and the barman — and not at my buddy — but a swing at the chick. So I took a swing at the barman: Me! You know?

TOM Missed.

MICHAEL Yeh. And then, the most marvellous choreographed movement, three more barmen vaulting over the counter and —

TOM You all ended up on your arses outside.

MICHAEL Yeh. And then —

TOM You all had to go back meekly for your overcoats . . . You told us ten years ago!

MICHAEL . . . Well, I was at this party the other night and I don't know what came over me, but I did something crazy.

TOM Yeh?

LIAM Yeh? —

JUNIOR Yeh? —

TOM Yeh? —

MICHAEL . . . No, forget that. But, ah, forget that, I was in the Village — you know? — one of those Village bars there recently and —

TOM No, the party the other night — you did something crazy

— What were you going to say?

MICHAEL Ah, that was nothing. But, one of those Village bars, and, and, listening to these two weirdos. One of them proving that Moses was in fact a stonecutter.

LIAM Proving it?

MICHAEL Proving it: dates, figures, blisters, the lot. And the other fella —

LIAM The Ten Commandments!

MICHAEL The other fella trying to get in with his own thesis, 'Yeah, man, I dig, man, but do you believe Jesus Christ committed suicide?'

TOM They're daft alright.

MICHAEL It was very funny.

LIAM And no one around to give one of them a box?

MICHAEL It was very funny.

JUNIOR Moses up the mountain chiselling away on the quiet behind a cloud.

MICHAEL It was very funny, Junie.

JUNIOR That's a good one.

But the general feeling is that it is not such a good one and there is a very brief pause.

LIAM But you're faring out well over there, Mick?

MICHAEL Yep.

LIAM Hah?

MICHAEL Oh, pretty good. I'm — I'm up for this part in a film, actually. And that tele a while back. And there's a possibility of a part in a stage play, but we don't know yet.

TOM 'We'? Who?

MICHAEL My agent.

TOM Oh, *you* have an agent?

MICHAEL I had an agent the last time I was home, what's wrong with an agent?

TOM I didn't say there was anything.

MICHAEL Everyone has an agent.

JUNIOR Begobs I haven't.

MICHAEL I'd say averaging ten — eleven grand over the past two/three years. That's not bad.

JUNIOR Not bad he says and the few quid a week my auld fella gives me. But I know how to diddle-dydle him on the petrol pumps.

MICHAEL What? Well, it's not bad. It's not good either. I know guys making fifty — a hundred grand a year.

JUNIOR I know fellas making nothing.

TOM So what? What are you telling us for?

MICHAEL Well, I wouldn't have made it clerking around here.

TOM You wouldn't.

JUNIOR Or teaching.

TOM What are you laughing at? — You wouldn't, you can say that again.

JUNIOR (*Laughing*) You could sing that, sir!

TOM Tck, Jack!

JUNIOR (*Guffawing*) As the bishop said to the actress!

TOM Shut up, you eejit!

JUNIOR (*Continues laughing/singing*) 'Sure no letter I'll be wearin', for soon will I be sailing — '(*To* MICHAEL) Hey, did you bring any home with yeh?

Laughter subsiding.

MICHAEL But I was in this place the other night.

TOM The party, is it?

MICHAEL No. Yes. But there was a guy there anyway —

TOM Who?

MICHAEL No, wait'll you hear this one, Tom. A fella, some nut, I didn't know him.

TOM Yeh?

LIAM Yeh? —

JUNIOR Yeh? —

TOM Yeh?

MICHAEL Well, he went a bit berserk anyway.

JUNIOR Beresk.

TOM Shh!

MICHAEL Well. He took off his clothes. (*He looks at them, unsure, his vulnerability showing; then he forces a laugh*) Well, he took off his clothes. Well, bollocks naked, jumping on tables and chairs, and then he started to shout 'No! No! This isn't it at all! This kind of — life — isn't it at all. Listen! Listen to me! Listen! I have something to tell you all!'

TOM Making his protest.

MICHAEL Yeh.

TOM Yeh?

MICHAEL Something to tell them all.

TOM Yeh?

MICHAEL Whatever — message — he had, for the world. And (*Moment's pause; then, simply*) Well. Then he tried to set himself on fire. (*He averts his eyes*)

LIAM Women there, Mick?

MICHAEL Yeh. (*Mustering himself again*) Ah, it wasn't anything serious — I mean, a party, a weirdo job. They were only laughing at him.

TOM Yeh?

MICHAEL Well, that's it. (*Forces a laugh*) They calmed him down — put out the flames, what?

TOM Yeh?

LIAM Yeh?

MICHAEL Oh yes, (*trying to laugh*) but then, then, one of the women took off *her* clothes and started cheering 'Up the Irish, up the I.R.A.!' What?

TOM (*Quietly*) His protest really foiled.

MICHAEL Yeh.

LIAM He was *Irish*?

MICHAEL What?

JUNIOR But what was up with him?

LIAM He was Irish?

MICHAEL Ah . . . yeh.

JUNIOR But what was up with him?

MICHAEL I don't know. Maybe someone put something in his drink or — There were all sorts of things going round — I mean, *we, we* were only laughing at him.

LIAM Did you know him, Mick?

MICHAEL I mean, I was drunk out of my skull myself.

TOM Yeh?

MICHAEL Well, that's it. Then he started crying, put on his clothes, I suppose, and left. I thought it was a good one.

LIAM Did you know him, Mick?

TOM Well that's a good one. (*Exchanges glances with* JUNIOR)

JUNIOR 'Tis.

29

MICHAEL I thought it was a good one.
LIAM Did he pull the quare one?
MICHAEL What?
LIAM The one that took off her clothes.
MICHAEL (*Extreme reaction*) Aw for Jesus' sake, Liam!
LIAM I was only joking.
TOM Well that's a good one.
JUNIOR 'Tis.
MICHAEL We need another round.

> PEGGY *has entered the front door and hallway. Now*
> *poking her head in lounge doorway. She is forty.*

PEGGY Hello, did he arrive, is he here, did he come? Ary how
yeh, Ridge, y'auld eejit yeh, you're as beautiful as ever,
janeymack you're looking delicious, you're as welcome
as the flowers in May!
MICHAEL Peggy.
PEGGY Look at you: gorgeous, and the suit!
MICHAEL You're looking well.
PEGGY Oh flattery, flattery! Holding my own.
MISSUS (*Appearing for a moment to see who has arrived*) Aaa —
PEGGY How long are you home for?
MICHAEL Oh —
MISSUS Peggy —
PEGGY How long? Hello, Missus —
MICHAEL Well —
PEGGY A few weeks?
MICHAEL Yeh. Well, we'll see.
PEGGY Well you're a sight for sore eyes, you didn't change a bit,
he's looking tip-top, isn't he?
TOM Will you sit down —
PEGGY Bejaneymack tonight, you're looking smashing.
TOM Will you sit down and don't be making a show of
yourself.

> *She sticks out her tongue at* TOM, *pokes a finger in his*
> *ribs and sits on the arm of his chair, stroking his hair.*
> TOM *making private world-weary faces to himself.*

PEGGY   When did you arrive?
MICHAEL   Last night.
PEGGY   Aa, did yeh?
MICHAEL   What are you having, Peggy?
PEGGY   Well, I'm going to have a gin and tonic in honour of yourself if his Nibs will allow me.
MICHAEL   Will we switch to shorts?
TOM   Oh? The Yank.
JUNIOR   The returned wank as the fella says.
MICHAEL   (*Calls*) The same again Missus, please!
TOM   (*Mocks belligerently — as is his style*) I'll have a whiskey.
JUNIOR   I'll stick to the pint.
LIAM   And a shot o' malt for me, Mike.
MICHAEL   Gin and tonic, Missus, three Scotch and a pint.
TOM   Irish!
MICHAEL   What?
TOM   Irish! Irish!
LIAM   And an Irish for me, Mike. Nothing but.
MICHAEL   One Scotch, Missus.
MISSUS   Thanks, thanks. Alright, Michael.
PEGGY   Well.

Short silence.

LIAM   'Around the fire one winter's night the farmer's rosy children sat.'
TOM   Oh?
PEGGY   It's nice to see us all together again, isn't it, it's like old times.
TOM   Isn't there a chair over there for yeh!
JUNIOR   (*Vacating his chair*) Here, a girleen.
PEGGY   (*Tongue out at* TOM, *a finger in his ribs*) Sourpuss! (*And takes* JUNIOR's *chair*)
JUNIOR   (*Belches*) Better out than your eye.
PEGGY   But tell us who you met over there, tell us all about the stars.
MICHAEL   Oh! (*Shrugs*)

Tom sighs.

31

PEGGY   Did you meet what's-his-name?
TOM   (*To himself*) Tck!
MICHAEL   You meet them all different times.
TOM   (*To himself*) Do yeh?
MICHAEL   Peter O'Toole.
PEGGY   Aa go on.
JUNIOR   (*Impressed*) Did yeh, did yeh though?
LIAM   Old Lawrence himself.
MICHAEL   Jack Lemmon.
PEGGY   And the other fella, the long fella?
MICHAEL   No.
JUNIOR   Did you ever meet —
MICHAEL   Paul Newman, Al Pacino.
PEGGY   Louis Jordan?
MICHAEL   Who?
TOM   Hopalong Cassidy. (*To* JUNIOR) Give us a cigarette.
JUNIOR   That big one, the Redgrave one — Veronica, is it?
TOM   (*Irritably*) Vanessa.
JUNIOR   Fine bird — Oosh! Big.
TOM   You must be a very popular fella over there, Michael.
JUNIOR   You must be a very familiar fella over there, sir.
TOM   (*Groans*) Isn't this awful.
JUNIOR   Jealousy will get you nowhere, Ryan.
TOM   D'yeh hear Jack, d'yeh hear Sonny, off-to-Palestine head. Palestine, was it, or the Congo, was it, Junie, you were going to a few years ago?
JUNIOR   You were the one always talking about travelling — JJ arranging things for you — you were the one was meant to be off doing the great things.
TOM   I never mentioned the Palestine Police Force.
JUNIOR   (*Laughing — as is the case with the others through the following*) I got married.
TOM   And look at the cut of you!
JUNIOR   Nice home, nice baba, nice wife, Gloria — (*Singing*) Oosh, she has a lovely bottom — set of teeth.
TOM   Ah but sure, what harm, your children will travel, your son will.
JUNIOR   He won't be a schoolmaster anyway.
TOM   An architect in Canada.
PEGGY   (*Laughing shrilly*) Oh yes, he was telling us one night.

TOM (*Philosophical sniff*) But d'ych see what I mean, the way the people are here: passing the buck. Twenty-seven years of age —

JUNIOR Thirty-one —

TOM And he's talking about what a five-month old son is going to do

JUNIOR Trotsky!

TOM Now! That's smiling Jack the Palestine Policeman!

JUNIOR Now! The great writer: Did ye read his great socialist piece in '*Boy's Own*'?

TOM Did you mend many carburettors today?

JUNIOR Did yous give many slaps today?

He drains his glass: MISSUS *is approaching with a tray of drinks. She serves* LIAM *first as usual.*

MISSUS Now, yas, that's the boy, Liam.

JUNIOR Off to write his great book.

LIAM Thank you, Mrs. Kilkelly.

JUNIOR But he had the first page wrote — the dedication, 'In gratitude to J. J. Kilkelly'.

TOM *reacts to this but bides his time.*

LIAM A nation of drop-outs as that professor said on the Late Late Show.

MISSUS When will we be seeing you on television, Michael, we do be watching?

MICHAEL Well, it's a question of whether the things I'm in are sold to here or —

But MISSUS *is already on her way back to the bar.*

MISSUS Your pint is on the way, Junior.

JUNIOR No hurry, Missus. (*Sighs, lamenting into his empty glass*)

TOM I never dedicated anything to anyone.

JUNIOR You never wrote anything.

TOM And I certainly never thought of dedicating anything to JJ.

JUNIOR Off to travel round the world to gain experience, and

33

look at him, lazier than Luke O'Brien's dog that has to
lean up against the wall to bark.

Big laugh.

PEGGY Well, cheers, Michael!
MICHAEL Good health, Peggy!
JUNIOR Cathaoireacha! (*Chairs*)
PEGGY (*To* MICHAEL) You're a tonic.
LIAM Good luck, fellas!
PEGGY You're just what we needed.
JUNIOR (*Again to his glass*) Yas.
PEGGY But tell us all.
MICHAEL Oh. You know?
PEGGY Aa go on now, tell us all. (TOM *groans*) What's up with
you tonight?
TOM 'Tell us all.' What does that mean?

Peggy looks away, hurt.

LIAM The sooner you two mavericks get hitched, the better.
TOM Did you hear the definition of the gentleman farmer? A
fella who bulls his own cows.
LIAM (*Through the laughter*) Ryan! . . . Ryan! One good heifer
any day is worth two months of a teacher's salary pound
for pound.
TOM Sterling or avoirdupois, Liam?

Off, the town clock ringing nine. MISSUS *approaching
with* JUNIOR's *pint.*

LIAM Ryan! Ryan! I made four hundred and twenty-eight
pounds on a single deal last week.
TOM At a puffed up auction.
JUNIOR God bless yeh, Missus.
LIAM What?
TOM Nothing. Good man.
MISSUS Now.

MICHAEL *has risen to pay for the round but* LIAM *is now*

34

awkwardly on his feet, bumping into JUNIOR, *in his haste.*

LIAM No! No! It's my round! I'm getting this!
JUNIOR (*Protecting his pint*) Jasus!
MICHAEL This one is mine, Liam —
LIAM No! No! Don't take anyone's money!
TOM He's getting carried away.
LIAM My round, fella!
MISSUS Sure it's alright, Liam.
LIAM (*To* MICHAEL) I've a question for you in a minute.
MISSUS Sure it's —
LIAM No! And have one yourself, Mrs. Kilkelly.
MISSUS No thanks, Liam, you're too good. (*Returning to bar*)
LIAM As a matter of fact my salary last year was — Well, it was
in excess — greatly in excess of any figure you
mentioned, boy. How much tax did you pay last year?
TOM Sit down!
LIAM How much!
JUNIOR Sit *down*!
LIAM For a little comparison, boy.
TOM Sit down outa that! —
JUNIOR For Jasus' sake! Good luck who stood!

MISSUS *returning with change for* LIAM.

MISSUS Now, Liam. That's the man.
PEGGY How's the lodger, Missus?
JUNIOR Josephine, wuw!

MISSUS *laughs, catering for them.*

PEGGY (*Aside to* MICHAEL) Were they telling you about the one?
MISSUS Aa but she's nice.
JUNIOR Very good-natured they say.
MISSUS But talking to the lads and her tea waiting on her in there
this two hours. (*Wandering out to front door*) That's who
I am waiting for now. (*Alone in front door*) D'ye know
now. (*Where she remains for some moments. And, off,
the church clock is chiming nine*)

35

PEGGY The place is gone to hell, isn't it?

MICHAEL I don't know. Not irreparably. But who put up that partition? This was all one room. Remember Tom, one of your socialist ideas to JJ. We were all very impressed: that there should be no public bar, no divisions or class distinctions.

LIAM What d'yeh mean, not irreparably, fella?

MICHAEL (*Not listening*) What? Get rid of that (*partition*) and see the space we'd have.

LIAM I wouldn't like to be the fella to inherit the debts of this place.

MICHAEL What are you on about all evening, Liam?

LIAM You're not fond of America, Mick?

MICHAEL This was our roots, Liam. This was to be our continuing cultural cradle: 'Let the word go forth from this time and place —' What? We could do it again! Wake up, wake up, boys and girls! — 'with a constant flow of good ideas.' (TOM *laughs/snorts at* MICHAEL's *romanticism*) What?

JUNIOR We could!

TOM Oh God, two of ye!

MICHAEL But doesn't it seem a pity?

LIAM That's okay, Mick —

MICHAEL Well, doesn't it?

TOM Create another pub?

MICHAEL It was more than a pub.

TOM Our culture, as indeed our nationalism, has always had the profoundest connections with the pub.

LIAM That's okay, fella, I'm keeping my eye on it quietly. I've the customer already on my books that it suits.

PEGGY Now. And poor Missus has other ideas. She thinks she has him earmarked for Anne.

LIAM (*Cockily — and he is drunker than the others*) I'm in no hurry for any Anne, or any other Anne (*To* MICHAEL) And, fella — fella! — that partition, out of the goodness of my pocket and my heart. Without obligation.

MICHAEL *looks at* TOM. TOM *has been waiting for him.*

TOM (*Blandly*) Yeh?

LIAM (*Laughs*) Unless, of course, you or your agent or your dollars would like me to handle the purchase for you. (*Sings in celebration of himself*) 'Put the blanket on the ground'! (*And drinks*)

MICHAEL *looks at* TOM *again.*

TOM (*Smiles blandly*) 'The torch has been passed to a new generation.'

JUNIOR (*Has been puzzling over a song to himself*) 'The sheep with their little lambs, passed me by on the road' — How does that begin?

TOM (*Still smiling blandly, cynically at* MICHAEL) Hmm?

JUNIOR That was JJ's song.

MICHAEL But. (*Drinks*) No, but, Annette, come to think of it now, she looks like JJ.

PEGGY Aa did you meet her? Isn't she a dote?

TOM That's an extraordinary observation, Michael, seeing you didn't recognise her when you saw her.

MICHAEL Aw, she does, does, look like JJ.

PEGGY But what has you home at this awful time of the year?

TOM Hope, refuge, to drink from his wellsprings, the romantic in his fancy suit.

MICHAEL It'd be no harm if you smartened yourself up a bit.

TOM (*Going to counter*) You'll have to do better than that. Missus! Give us a packet of cigarettes. Ten Carrolls.

JUNIOR (*Still trying to work it out*) 'The sheep with their little lambs passed me on the road'.

MICHAEL What's your news, Peggy, they told me nothing.

PEGGY Did they tell you we have a new priest?

MICHAEL No. What's he like?

TOM Ridiculous. Jesus, the last fella was bad, Father Benny Diction Connolly was a snob, but at least that's something: this fella is an eejit.

PEGGY For as much as you see of the church to know what he is.

TOM Ah, but I went to check him out. My dear brethren — This was his sermon one Sunday. (*A warning to* PEGGY) Don't interrupt me now. A maan (*man*) wan time, wan place, somewhere, that kept leaving the church before the maas (*Mass*) was ended, and continued this maalpractice though repeatedly warned about it. An' wan Sunday, my dear brethern, wasn't he sloppin' outa the church wance again, an' just as he was steppin' outside didn't he look up at the clock to see what time 'twas, and d'yeh know what happened to him? — d'ye know what happened to him! The church clock fell off the tower on top of him. Now! Killed stone dead.

PEGGY Oh that's exaggerated, love.

TOM Ridiculous. In this day and age! And the young ones are worse, falling over backwards, arse over elbow, to talk about sex to show how progressive they are. Sex: progressive — Jesus! — Ridiculous — Smoke? (*To* JUNIOR)

PEGGY You never see any good in the Church.

TOM Aa but I do, love. Look at Liam there, and he's a regular churchgoer. And think of how the marriage figures all over the country would have slumped again only for all the young nuns jumping over the wall and the young priests waiting for them outside with their cassocks lifted.

PEGGY Oh that's not right.

TOM Ridiculous. Tell us something, Ridge, anything, something interesting, for God's sake.

PEGGY . . . You got quiet or something, Michael. Tell us how are all the girls treating you? Oh, there was a rumour some time back — Wasn't there, love? — that you were married.

MICHAEL No.

PEGGY What?

MICHAEL I answered that one.

PEGGY What?

MICHAEL Well, there was a girl — some time back. I knew her quite well — intimately — know what I mean? She was working in this night club, and this guy starts chatting her up, charming her, et cetera.

LIAM Yeh?

JUNIOR Big bird?

MICHAEL But this guy, he had a few bucks anyway, a yacht and all that, and he was trying to persuade her to go off on a trip with him.

JUNIOR Yi-yi!

MICHAEL   That's the point. Eventually she did, the two of them alone on the boat for three weeks and he never tried to make her, never laid a hand on her. And she committed suicide.

TOM   Ary Ridge!

MICHAEL   I thought that would be your reaction.

LIAM   What?

TOM   Tck!

PEGGY   (*Smiling/frowning*) Did she drown herself or what, Michael?

LIAM   A good boot in the arse she wanted.

MICHAEL   He was a sadist or something.

JUNIOR   He was a gomey if you ask me.

TOM   And what's to signify in that story?

MICHAEL   I knew her. She was — a friend. And I knew him.

TOM   (*Rising*) Ridiculous country. The luck is on me I never left here. (*Calls*) You might as well start filling the acthoring man's round, Missus!

MICHAEL   Better make them doubles.

TOM   Oh?

MICHAEL   Some people need the stimulation.

TOM *laughs and exits to the Gents.*

PEGGY   But you must go into a lot of queer places over there?

MICHAEL   Maybe they'd be only 'queer' to people from round here.

MISSUS   Doubles, Michael?

MICHAEL   Yes! Why not!

PEGGY   Oh, did they tell you they nearly marched on the North one night?

MISSUS   And a pint for you, Junior?

JUNIOR   Aye-Aye, Missus.

PEGGY   Did they tell you?

LIAM   You're not a political animal, Mike?

MICHAEL   Excuse me, Liam, but no one round here ever called me Mick, Mike or Mickeen, okay?

LIAM *nods, gravely bovine.* MICHAEL *offering cigarettes around.* PEGGY *accepts one unconsciously.* JUNIOR *singing snatches of 'All in the April Evening'.*

PEGGY But you're getting on well over there?
MICHAEL Strugglin'. Smoke, Junie?
PEGGY Aa go on —
JUNIOR Thanks boy —
PEGGY But are yeh getting on well though?
MICHAEL Yep.
LIAM Never use 'em.
PEGGY But seriously, are you? (*He is lighting her cigarette*)
MICHAEL Yes.
JUNIOR 'The sheep with their little lambs . . .'
PEGGY Oh I didn't want this at all. (*But she puffs away at it*) But do yeh like it all the time?
MICHAEL (*Irritably*) Yes, Peggy, it's marvellous.
PEGGY I see.
MICHAEL And how are things with you?
PEGGY Oh now.
MICHAEL What?
PEGGY Oh indeed.
MICHAEL Yes?
PEGGY Oh now, don't ask me.
MICHAEL You gave up the dressmaking, didn't you?
PEGGY Well, yeh know, around here.
MICHAEL And the singing?
PEGGY What singing? (*Remembering, laughing shrilly*) Oh yes! JJ and his classical music, and he having me up to the nuns taking singing lessons. Wasn't I the eejit? And wait'll I tell yeh, (*whispering*) I had a crush on him. That slob. And he old enough to be my father. I'm not saying anything, it was all in innocence. And Sister Jerome, the singing teacher, tone deaf.
JUNIOR 'Passed me by on the road.'
MICHAEL Who was the slob?
PEGGY JJ! Wait'll Tom comes back. (*He'll tell you*)
MICHAEL So, you're minding the house with your mother?
PEGGY Oh but I do a morning or two a week, now and again, bookkeeping for the vet.
MICHAEL And how is that old friend of yours, Helen Collins?
PEGGY Isn't she married? Sure you must have known — She's producing like mad. Well, three and one on the way, as they say. But she's let herself go to hell — Hasn't she,

40

Junie? — I'm meant to look like her daughter and she's ten months younger than me.

MICHAEL I see.

PEGGY But sure you must have known, wasn't she an old flame of yours? (*She pauses for only the briefest moment not wanting to acknowledge the thought that he has been getting at her*) Oh but they're hopefully going to open a tourist office here next year — Isn't that right, Liam? — and I'm in the running for it (*a smile at* LIAM) if I know the right people. (*Then smiling bravely, a glance at* MICHAEL, *then averts her eyes.* MICHAEL *feeling ashamed of himself, looks at her empty glass and his own*)

MICHAEL That's — That's great. Hang on.

He goes to the counter and returns with his own and PEGGY'S *drink.*

LIAM An' so was Beethoven, fellas. Stone deaf.

MICHAEL (*Toasting* PEGGY) The best! Those curtains are yours.

PEGGY And I was up all night finishing them. And never got paid.

MICHAEL We didn't want to get paid.

PEGGY (*Impulsively, she throws her arms around him*) Ary, yeh daft auld romantic, it's lovely to see yeh! Oh gosh-golly, this is gone out again.

MICHAEL *relights her cigarette.* MISSUS *approaching with* TOM'S *and* LIAM'S *drinks.*

MISSUS I'll clear a few of these glasses out of yer way now.

JUNIOR And the pint, Missus.

MISSUS That's coming, Junior.

JUNIOR *sighs to himself.*

PEGGY And d'yeh know? I could whistle the whole of the Sixth Symphony from beginning to end.

TOM (*Returning from Gents*) They're daft alright.

PEGGY Stop now, we were having a lovely time while you were out.

TOM But do you yourself take questions like that seriously now?

PEGGY Cheers, Michael!

MICHAEL Cheers!

LIAM Luck, fellas!

TOM Michael?

MICHAEL Questions like what?

LIAM Questions like did Jesus Ch— Did you-know-who commit suicide.

TOM And questions of the immoral and unethical behaviour of not screwing a bird on a boat. (MISSUS *returning to the bar*) And, as Liam so delicately put it, for the propriet-ress's and my fiancée's sensitivities no doubt, questions like do you believe did you-know-who commit suicide.

MICHAEL What's up with you?

TOM (*Philosophical sniff*) Aw now.

JUNIOR (*To himself*) Aw fuck this! — Missus! — (*Striding to the bar, frustrated by his empty glass*) Give me a drop of the hard tack too, and as well as the pint you're filling *now* you might start filling *another* pint for whoever is buying the next round.

MICHAEL What's up with you?

TOM Aw now.

PEGGY You've changed, Michael.

MICHAEL *I've* changed?

PEGGY You used to be a grand shy lad with just the odd old, yeh know, flourish.

TOM And supercilious with it.

MICHAEL Well, I never nearly marched on the North, and I never thought a bank clerk is any more ridiculous for what she does than anybody else, and I never thought the jack-boot in the arse was the cure for everything, and I never thought —

LIAM Hold it, fella —

MICHAEL That you (*Tom*) did either.

LIAM Right there, fella —

MICHAEL And to think of it!

LIAM Fella!

MICHAEL We were going to change all this!

LIAM Fella!

42

TOM You're missing the point —

MICHAEL In this very room! And now it's bollocks talk about Protestants.

TOM No one said anything about —

MICHAEL The great anti-cleric (*Tom*) nearly going off to fight a Holy War!

TOM No one said anything about —

LIAM A minority Catholic group being oppressed!

MICHAEL You must be very unhappy in your lives —

TOM Nothing to do with clerics —

LIAM Fella! —

TOM It's your ridiculous attitude —

LIAM Brave Irish Catholic men and women —

MICHAEL Everything seems ridiculous to you.

TOM Women and sex orgies and some myth in your mind about JJ —

LIAM Because — because a discriminating majority —

MICHAEL You're really into 1917.

TOM What's all this about JJ?

LIAM A discriminating and — And! — gerrymandering majority! —

MICHAEL Back to the stuck-in-the-mud-festering ignorance!

TOM 'Wellsprings and lost horizons'! —

MICHAEL Yes! —

LIAM A gerrymandering! —

MICHAEL Lost horizons!

LIAM Fella, fella! A gerrymandering majority! —

TOM Never arriving at reality.

LIAM You can't deny it, you can't deny it — And! —

TOM All mixed up —

LIAM And! Racial memory, boy!

TOM Stop, Liam —

LIAM Deny that one, boy!

TOM Stop. Liam!

LIAM Cause you can't deny it! — And! — And! — You can't deny it!

TOM Stop!

LIAM Cause — cause! — Fella! — Fella! —

TOM Stop-stop-stop!

LIAM You can't deny it!

TOM Stop, will you, Liam! — Stop! — Forget that.

LIAM I will not forget it! (*Forgetting it*) I will not forget it.

TOM You and your kind with your rose-coloured lights that you can switch on and off so easily. You don't want reality.

MICHAEL Well, if yours is the reality.

TOM Oh?

MICHAEL Reality is always about poverty, is it?

TOM No, it's always about flowers. Look, excuse me, Michael —

But LIAM *is off again.*

LIAM And there's a thing called Truth, fella — you may not have heard of it. And Faith, fella. And Truth and Faith and Faith and Truth inex — inextricably — inextricably bound. And-And! — cultural heritage — you may not (have) heard of it — No border, boy! And cultural heritage inex-inextricably bound with our Faith and Hope and Hope and Faith and *Truth*! And some of us, and some of us, at least, cherish and — cherish and — and — are not supercilious, boy, with it — about it. Fella. I will not forget it! Last refuge in Europe.

TOM Fine, Liam, rest yourself now.

JUNIOR (*In answer to a glance from* LIAM) Well spoken, boy.

TOM Look, excuse me, Michael, but what is the point, the real issue of what we are discussing?

MICHAEL Well, maybe I have changed, because my enjoyment in life comes from other things than recognising my own petty malice in others.

TOM Is that the point?

MICHAEL A simple matter — and it's not a dream — of getting together and doing what we did before.

TOM Is that the point? To do what we did before? Tell me, what did we do before?

MICHAEL To do what we did before.

TOM (*To himself*) Jesus! Extraordinary how the daft romantics look back at things.

MICHAEL Why is everyone calling me a romantic?

TOM It's more polite.

MICHAEL You would never have made the statements you are
making tonight a few years ago.

LIAM I'd reckon, fella, that proves he ain't static.

MICHAEL It depends on which direction he went.

LIAM I'd reckon, fella, that you are all — (washed-up)

TOM No. Hold on. I think you're serious, Michael, hmm? I
think he's serious. I think we have *another* leader.
Another true progressive on our hands at last, lads.
Another white fuckin' liberal.

PEGGY Shh, love.

TOM Home to re-inspire us, take a look at our problems,
shake us out of our lethargy, stop us vegetating, show us
where we went wrong —

MICHAEL You're choosing the words —

TOM Show us that we're not forgotten, bringing his new suici-
dal fuckin' Christ with him.

PEGGY Love —

MICHAEL Vegetating, lethargy, forgotten —

TOM And most surprisingly, I think the poor hoor — like his
illustrious predecessor — does not know where he is
himself.

MICHAEL (*Laughs*) I've been having a great time —

TOM No — No!

MICHAEL Marvellous time!

TOM You're too depressed, Jack, too much on the defensive,
Jack —

MICHAEL Marvellous! But cheers anyway, Jack, cheers!

TOM The point, Michael, the real point and issue for you,
Michael — D'yeh want to hear? You came home to stay,
to *die*, Michael.

LIAM Correct.

TOM And fair enough, do that, but be warned, we don't want
another JJ.

MICHAEL (*Laugh/smile is gone*) I never mentioned I had any inten-
tion of staying home.

LIAM Correct.

MICHAEL What do you know about JJ?

LIAM Enough, fella. But leave it to me, I'll rescue this place
shortly.

MICHAEL You spent so much of your time away as a student, the

story was they were going to build a house for you in the
university.

TOM Michael.

MICHAEL And you know nothing about JJ either.

TOM I'm marking your card for you. JJ is a slob.

MICHAEL He —

TOM A slob —

MICHAEL Wasn't —

TOM Is, was, always will be. A slob. He's probably crying and
slobbering on somebody's shoulder now this minute,
somewhere around Galway. Missus in there treats him as
if he were a child.

JUNIOR (*Angrily, rising*) And what else can the woman do?

TOM I'm just telling him.

JUNIOR (*Exits to Gents*) Jesus!

MICHAEL Why?

TOM Why what?

MICHAEL Why are you telling me — and glorying in it?

TOM JJ is a *dangerous* and weak slob. He limped back from
England, about 1960. England was finished for him. He
couldn't face it again. I hope this is not ringing too many
bells for you personally. And he would have died from
drink, or *other* things, but for the fact that the John F.
Kennedy show had started on the road round about
then, and some auld woman in the town pointed out
doesn't he look like John F. Kennedy. And JJ hopped up
on the American-wrapped bandwagon of so-called
idealism —

MICHAEL He had his own idealism.

TOM Until he began to think he *was* John F. Kennedy.

MICHAEL And, in a way, he was.

TOM And Danny O'Toole up the road thinks he's Robert
Mitchum and he only five feet two?

MICHAEL He re-energised this whole town.

TOM And Danny O'Toole is winning the west for us? Then
people started to look at our new slob-hero afresh.
People like Missus in there — she pinned her hopes on
him — and, he quickly hopped up on her too. And so
became the possessor of her premises, which we, and
others put together for him, restyled at his dictates into

46

a Camelot, i.e. a thriving business for selling pints.

MICHAEL No —

TOM Alright, selling pints was a secondary consideration. Like all Camelot-pub owners he would have welcomed a clientele of teetotallers. His real purpose of course was to foster the arts, to give new life to broken dreams and the horn of immortality, nightly, to mortal men . . . But then came the fall.

MICHAEL The assassination.

TOM Of whom?

MICHAEL Kennedy.

TOM Oh I thought for a minute there you were talking about *our* president, JJ.

MICHAEL Well.

TOM What?

MICHAEL Well, as I heard it, after Kennedy's death, the *character-assassination* of JJ started in earnest.

TOM No.

MICHAEL Well, as you said yourself earlier, the priest's visits, other people's visits and the people the priest represented.

TOM No. After Kennedy's assassination, the grief, yes. We all experienced it. But is grief a life-long profession?

MICHAEL A lot of people feared and hated JJ in this town.

TOM Feared? No. Never.

MICHAEL Well, even on the evidence of tonight one could easily get the impression that this town could have had a few things — just a few, Tom? — to do with 'our' president's fall.

TOM No! Look, he hopped up on that load of American straw and he had so little going for him that when that load of straw went up in smoke, JJ went up with it. No! Oh yes, they hated him — Why wouldn't they: Puppetry, mimicry, rhetoric! What had he to offer anyone? Where were the facts, the definitions?

MICHAEL Why are you getting so excited?

TOM I'm not getting excited. He-fed-people's-fantasies. That's all he did. Fed — people's — fantasies.

MICHAEL People are afraid of realising themselves.

TOM Look, look, look — lookit! — (*To himself*) Shit!

MICHAEL They fear that.

47

TOM Realising themselves? Like you did? Look! — Lookit! — leaving aside the superficial fact that he looked like John F. Kennedy — somewhere around the left ball — he could just as easily have thought he was John McCormack or Pope John. He had so little going for him and we are such a ridiculous race that even our choice of assumed images is quite arbitrary.

MICHAEL Are you finished?

TOM The only mercy in the whole business, as I see it, is that he did not in fact think he was John McCormack.

LIAM Man, Tomeen!

MICHAEL JJ's respect, opinion and esteem for you —

TOM To thine own self be true? God we're a glorious people alright.

LIAM C'rrect.

LIAM *has risen and is going to Gents.*

TOM Look, don't fret yourself about not seeing him tonight —

MICHAEL I haven't given up on seeing him tonight.

TOM (*Groans*) Aw Lord. There are plenty of JJs about. (*Pointing at* LIAM *who is exiting to Gents*) I prefer that.

MICHAEL You won't listen to my interpretation?

PEGGY Aa, lads.

TOM By all means — if you have one.

MICHAEL JJ's opinion of you —

TOM And if it's a sensible one.

MICHAEL The *esteem* he held you in, always, way above the rest of us —

TOM Ah-ah-ah-ah! Don't try that one. Remember where you are now. It's clear from the way you've been talking all night that the — innocence — naiveté of New York has softened your head, but you're talking to the people of a little town in the west of Ireland now. A little more sophisticated than that for us, Michael.

MICHAEL JJ and his wife, his first wife, were walking along a street, and —

TOM In England?

MICHAEL Yes.

PEGGY Lads.

TOM Just making sure I'm following facts.

MICHAEL And a car came along, the steering was perfect, the driver was sober, but the driver was some poor unhappy bitter little prick who wanted to kill someone, anyone, and he drove the car up on the footpath and knocked JJ's wife over, and she died in hospital three months later.

TOM Yes.

MICHAEL And that's what you describe as the 'limp' JJ came into this town with?

TOM Yes.

MICHAEL What do you mean 'yes'?

TOM Yes. I heard that story, and I'm sorry for him — if it's true.

MICHAEL What?

TOM No-no-no. Look, there are a lot of things we heard and believed some years ago, but we're a little older now.

MICHAEL A man — after a tragedy like that —

TOM More interesting stories are emerging now about JJ's past.

MICHAEL To pull himself together after a tragedy like that and start afresh.

TOM Look, I don't recall anybody ever reading any headlines about the tragic and dramatic event.

PEGGY He made it up, Michael.

TOM (*To* PEGGY) Keep out of it — And people are now of the opinion that JJ was never married before, that there was no first wife, that there was only a bird, that there was no —

MICHAEL Jesus, you're exceeding yourself! What's happened to you?

TOM Alright, there *was* an accident! — and you can drag your own limp into it and your own grandmother as well — but it does not change the fact of the point we are *now* discussing, which is that JJ is, was, always will be a slob. Now, can you contradict me?

MICHAEL I like him.

TOM A-a-a-w! Back to the flowers. How nice, how fey, how easy for you. 'I like him'. And the way he upset and thwarted and wilfully and irresponsibly inflated and abused people. When I think of it. 'Together let us explore the stars.' Jesus!

> JUNIOR *comes out of the Gents: his hand up for attention: he has got the first line of the song.*

JUNIOR I've got it! 'All in the April Evening'.
TOM (*To himself*) And left them high and dry.
PEGGY (*Catering for him*) And bills outstanding all over the country, love, didn't he?

> *An angry grimace/gesture from* TOM: *he does not want her comments. Junior — this is not his game — goes to the bar and stays there for some moments.*

JUNIOR Missus! Throw us out that other pint.
TOM God, we're a glorious people alright. Half of us, gullible eejits, people like yourself, ready to believe in anything. And the other half of us —
MICHAEL People like yourself, ready to believe nothing.
TOM People like yourself — people like yourself — ready to believe, get excited, follow to the death any old bollocks with a borrowed image, any old JJ who has read a book on American politics or business methods. Jesus, images: fuckin' neon shadows.
PEGGY Love.
MICHAEL And the other half of us ready to believe in nothing.
TOM No! You don't understand! Never the sound, decent, honest-to-God man for us. Never again in this world, for us, or for anyone else.

> JUNIOR *joins them.*

JUNIOR Good luck, fellas.

> *Silence.*

MICHAEL (*Quietly*) He nearly made it.
TOM 'Nearly'? I thought you were knocking us for that word a few minutes ago?
MICHAEL He was great.

TOM In what way? When? — How? — Where — Convince me! — Tell me!

MICHAEL He hadn't got over the first knock when the second happened.

TOM Isn't that my proof, isn't that the test of a man? Sure all you're mentioning is his — dubious — misfortunes and some kind of hypothetical potential. What did he achieve? What was he talking about?

MICHAEL I don't know what he was talking about, but he was right.

TOM That's fine, you don't know, that concludes the matter.

MICHAEL Did you believe too much in him?

TOM Now, I like that. You're coming up to our standards after all.

MICHAEL Do you feel he let you down personally or what?

TOM The gentle romantic has his subtly nasty side.

MICHAEL Did you hope too much in him? — Was he your only life-line?

TOM No, I didn't hope too much in him, and I never ran messages for him or fell flat on my face for him.

MICHAEL He didn't ask you to —

TOM Bloody sure he didn't.

MICHAEL Because you were the — doyen? — of his group.

TOM I wouldn't have minded him succeeding — but I had him taped from the start.

JUNIOR (*A warning that* MISSUS *has appeared*) Yas, enough dialectics as the fella said.

> *But* MISSUS *has come outside the bar-counter to inter-cept* LIAM *who is entering from the Gents and slip him a drink on the house and have a fawning word with him.*

TOM I can see you're not the wide-eyed boy who left here —

MICHAEL Thanks —

TOM But since you have nothing to offer but a few distorted memories, and a few personal tricks on the burning monk caper, I'm marking your card. You've come home to stay, die, whatever — and you're welcome — but save us the bullshit. We've had that from your predecessor. We won't put up with it again. Don't try to emulate him, no re-energising, cultural cradles or stirring that old pot. Now I know you have it in you to take my caution and take the security of following more careful steps.

MICHAEL Are you threatening me?

TOM Holy Moses, Michael! — Me twin! — We don't threaten anyone. We don't have to! All we have to do — all we ever had to do — is wait! (*He laughs*) We leave it at that? God bless you.

MICHAEL I'm not sure what I came home for, but I think I'm finding out.

LIAM *and* MISSUS *joining them.*

LIAM Leave that matter to me, Mrs. Kilkelly.

MISSUS Better looking this man (*Liam*) is getting every day, isn't he? D'ye know now. Yas. You didn't bring a blondie home with you, Michael?

MICHAEL There are dark-haired girls in America too, Missus.

MISSUS Musha, God help them. Be careful of them American ladies, a mac (*son*).

MICHAEL (*Pointedly looking about*) How's business, Missus?

MISSUS Oh, well, now, the off-season. Isn't that it, Liam?

LIAM That is c'rrect, Mrs. Kilkelly.

MISSUS And things'll be picking up for us soon. Now.

MICHAEL What you should do is get in a few of the natives telling funny stories for the tourists, and singing. And when things get going you could move out with the family and live in the henhouse for the season.

MISSUS Isn't that what they're doing, some of them, living with the hens, to make room for tourists. And some of them, Michael —

MICHAEL Yes. I didn't pay you for that last round.

MICHAEL *is standing, a roll of money in his hand.* MISSUS *feels offended by his cutting her short.*

MISSUS Five pounds and sixty-nine pence. Yas, your mother is delighted: I was talking to her for a minute this morning in the post office and she drawing out a wad of money. (*All get the implications of her remark. She gives* MICHAEL

change out of her cardigan pocket) Thanks, Michael.
That's the woman with the money.
JUNIOR Looking for a girl he is, Missus, wasn't he admiring the
daughter?
MISSUS Aa, Annette.
PEGGY Aa, she's a dote. What's she going to do, Missus?
JUNIOR I bet she wants to be an air hostess.
MISSUS The cute Junior: how did you know that now?
JUNIOR Oh-oh!
MISSUS No. We were thinking of the bank. (*A glance at* LIAM)
Well, for the meanwhile, that is.
JUNIOR Speak of an angel!
PEGGY Oh hello, Anne.
ANNE (*Silently*) Hello.

> ANNE *has come in. She moves aside with* MISSUS *to
> report briefly in a whisper — little more than a shake of
> her head. (She has not found her father)* MISSUS
> *contains a sigh.*

PEGGY The lovely coat.
MISSUS And any sign of Josephine?
ANNE She's up in Daly's lounge. She said she had a sandwich
and not to bother with her tea.
MISSUS Alright.

> MISSUS *wanders off, out to the front door, sighs out at
> the night, then exits upstairs. And, meanwhile,* ANNE *is
> taking off her coat and moving to attend the bar.*

TOM Anne! Come 'ere a minute. D'yeh know our acthoring
man, Michael Ridge?
MICHAEL D'yeh not remember me? (*She has a natural shyness but
it does not efface an interest she has in him*) Hmm?
ANNE I do.
MICHAEL What?
ANNE I remember you here with Daddy.
MICHAEL How is he?
ANNE Not so good. (*She looks up at him, gravely, simply, for
his reaction. He nods, simply, his understanding. Then*

53

she smiles) You're welcome home. (*And they shake hands*)

TOM (*Without malice*) Gee, kid, you were only so high when I saw you last.

MICHAEL Is it Anne or Annette? (*She shrugs: her gesture meaning that the choice is his*) Anne. (*She nods, smiles, a silent 'okay'*) You're finished school?

ANNE Three months time.

MICHAEL And you won't be sorry.

ANNE No. (*And she laughs*)

PEGGY Dreadful people, the nuns. Dreadful. Sister Bartholomew is the worst, don't you think, Anne?

ANNE Isn't she dead?

PEGGY (*Laughing shrilly*) Oh God yes, I forgot! I'm awful. But they're dreadful tyrants.

ANNE *is already moving away.*

MICHAEL Will you come back and join us?

ANNE (*A toss of her head, smiling back at him*) I might.

TOM Is it Anne or Annette, Michael?

MICHAEL And she *is* like JJ. Well, things are looking up!

JUNIOR Will we go up and have a few in Paddy Joe Daly's?

MICHAEL The opposition, the enemy? No! We're grand here now.

JUNIOR We'll introduce you to Josephine —

TOM ⎫ Grrrrah!
JUNIOR ⎭ Grrrrah!

PEGGY But were they telling you about the one? And the hair? And the walk?

MICHAEL Red hair? Frizzed out? I saw her crossing the street near the bank when I was driving my mother today.

PEGGY The most ridiculous thing that ever hit this town — isn't she, love?

MICHAEL I was wondering who she was. She's a fine-looking bird.

JUNIOR (*His appreciation again for large ladies*) She's big.

PEGGY Excuse me —

JUNIOR No bother there, sham.

MICHAEL No! Anne! Hope!

TOM God!

PEGGY Excuse me. That girl (*Josephine*) is a fine-looking — !

54

MICHAEL Hmm?
PEGGY I'm disappointed in you, Michael.
LIAM Dirty aul' thing.
JUNIOR I hear she fancies you, cowboy.
PEGGY (*At* MICHAEL) Tck!
MICHAEL What?
PEGGY Your taste. That girl.
MICHAEL I'm not interested in her.
TOM Gee, tough luck on Josephine.
PEGGY (*Neurotically*) She's a disgusting girl, she's stupid — Did you see her neck?
MICHAEL I only said —
PEGGY Of course you didn't. Everyone is talking about her, she won't last long here. She wouldn't even be kept in this place only for it's up to its eyes in debt.
TOM What's up with yeh?
PEGGY Every man in the town, married and single, around her, like — like terriers.
TOM What's up with yeh?
PEGGY Ary I get sick of this marvellous stuff. Everything is 'marvellous' with Ridge.
MICHAEL I only said —
PEGGY Everything is 'marvellous' —
MICHAEL Alright she isn't marvellous —
PEGGY Everything is 'marvellous' —
TOM What are ye — what's —
MICHAEL But she's good-looking, good legs —
PEGGY Everything is 'marvellous' —
JUNIOR Jugs (*tits*) —
MICHAEL She has a good job —
JUNIOR Bottom —
PEGGY Will she keep it — Will she keep it?
MICHAEL Sexy-looking —
PEGGY I don't agree, I don't agree!
TOM Wait a minute —
PEGGY I don't agree!
TOM Hold on a minute —
PEGGY Why should I agree?
TOM What are ye talking about!
LIAM She's a dirty aul' thing!

55

TOM (*Silencing them*) What-are-ye-on-about! (*To* PEGGY) What are you squealin' about?

PEGGY (*Laughs suddenly, shrilly*) Ary shut up the lot of ye!

TOM Are you finished? She's ridiculous alright.

PEGGY Of course, she is —

TOM And you're worse! The whole town is filled with — pookies.

LIAM Strangers comin' in to run the town, fellas.

TOM (*Groans to himself; then*) Anne! Annette! Missus! Where are they? Pint, gin, tonic, Scotch, two Irish! (*He feels* MICHAEL's *eyes on him*) Yeh?

MICHAEL Why don't you leave?

TOM But I might lose my religion.

PEGGY What's he (*Michael*) saying?

MICHAEL You can still get out.

TOM But what of my unfinished work here? My feverish social writings. Whose red pen would in merit and logic stand up to the passionate lucidity of Fr. O'Mara's sermons? Would you take my place, take me from my great vocation, and send me off to be setting myself on fire in the great adventure of the New World?

MICHAEL There's still time.

PEGGY What's *he* saying?

TOM I've always taken my responsibilities seriously.

PEGGY Of course you have, love.

TOM *gesturing, rolling his head in reaction to her.*

MICHAEL What responsibilities for Christ's —

TOM My mother, Jack, for Christ's sake, and my father, Jack, for Christ's sake. You enquired about my mother's health earlier but, for some strange reason or other, not my father's. Well, I can asssure you they're both still alive. (*To* LIAM) Don't be making wild-life faces at me, cowboy, I've got the goods on you.

LIAM Didn't say a thing, fella.

Off, the town clock chiming ten.

MICHAEL Do you know what he said about you one evening?

56

TOM Who? (*Closes his eyes tightly; he doesn't want to know*)
Oh yes, our president.

MICHAEL That if you didn't break out of it, none of us would.

TOM (*Continues with eyes shut*) Break out of what?

MICHAEL This.

TOM Are you speaking geographically.

MICHAEL Not necessarily. This talk all evening, and what it seems to represent?

TOM What does it represent?

MICHAEL You'd think the sixties never happened.

TOM What did the sixties represent?

MICHAEL Not this.

TOM You-haven't-answered-a-single-question-all-night. You, too, are a great dealer in the abstract.

MICHAEL The social movements of the minority's groups in the sixties, in towns, villages and cities, was the rising culture.

TOM And *is* the *rising* culture, begod!

ANNE *arrives with a tray of drinks.*

ANNE Scotch, Michael?

TOM Ah, God bless yeh, Anne — Because despite the current swing to the right of the majorities, and the crusades of the christian fundamentalist majorities, promoting medieval notions of morality and reality, begod —

JUNIOR ⎫ Thanks, girl —

TOM ⎭ We the creative minorities are still here, begod, thank God, swinging to the left while they're swinging to the right. But we, the swinging-to-the-lefters will see those swinging-to-the-righters go swinging to their decline and disintegration — For! — And! — As you say! — even though we are the minority, it is always out of the creative cultural minority groups that change irrevocable comes about! Begod! What do you think of that? (*To* MICHAEL) Happy? He's not happy still — begod! And why would he? I left out the big one. (*He is searching his pockets for money for the round*)

LIAM Good luck, fellas.

Off, the church clock is chiming ten.

TOM   Because — fellas! — despite us, the representatives of the rising cultural minorities aforementioned, what is going on now, this minute, ablow in Paddy Joe Daly's? 'Put th' fuckin' blanket on the ground.' (*They laugh*) But Paddy Joe Daly is not the enemy. He may personify it, the bullets in his bandy legs may symbolise it, the antics of his lump of a wife may dramatise it. But no — No! — the real enemy — the big one! — that we shall overcome, is the country-and-western system itself. Unyielding, uncompromising, in its drive for total sentimentality. A sentimentality I say that would have us all an unholy herd of Sierra Sues, sad-eyed inquisitors, sentimental Nazis, fascists, sectarianists, black-and-blue shirted nationalists, with spurs a-jinglin', all ridin' down the trail to Oranmore. Aw great, I knew I'd make ye all happy.

      They laugh.

JUNIOR   Aw, Jasus, the twins. (*He slips the money for the round to* ANNE)
MICHAEL   Do you ever go for rambles down to Woodlawn like we used to, Anne?
ANNE   Sometimes.

      And she moves off to answer a tapping on the counter in the public bar — a toss of her head and a smile back at MICHAEL.

JUNIOR   The two of ye together might make up one decent man.
TOM   Well, whatever about me, I don't know what reason you had to hang around here, Sonny.
JUNIOR   We've had the complimenting stage, let that be an end to the insulting stage, and we'll get on to the singing stage. (*Singing*) 'All in the April evening' —
TOM   And your father won't leave you the garage. One of the young brothers will have that.
JUNIOR   (*Smile disappears*) They can have it so they can.
TOM   They will.

58

LIAM   And that's the belief in the town.

JUNIOR   (*Back in form*) No! No! They're all off, the whole seven of them, to join the Palestine Police Force next week. Wuw! Off like Jewish foreskins! Jasus, Jasus . . . ! Come on, Peggy, you're the singer here.

PEGGY   Oh stop, Junior.

JUNIOR   Come on, that one, JJ's song —

PEGGY   I don't know when I sang last.

JUNIOR   'All in the April evening, April airs —'

PEGGY   Stop, Junie. No. No —

JUNIOR ⎱ 'The sheep with their little lambs —' Come on!

PEGGY ⎰ No, no, no, no, no —

JUNIOR ⎱ Come on, come on —

PEGGY ⎰ No, no, no, no, no —

LIAM   (*About to sing*) Fellas!

> But PEGGY *is standing up; she sings the first line of 'All in the April Evening'; then giggling; then fixing herself into the pose of the amateur contralto at the wedding, and singing deliberately off key and 'poshly' distorting the words.*

PEGGY   'All in the April evening' — No, wait a minute . . . . 'This is my lovely dee. This is thee dee I shall remember the dee' — Christina Jordan, did you ever hear her? — 'I'll remember, I'll remember — !' The cheek of her, not a note right in her head — 'I'll remember, I'll remember — ' Jeeney! The eejit. (*And she sits abruptly, hands over her mouth, giggling*)

LIAM   Fellas! (*Fancies himself as a cowboy singer*) 'There's a bridle hanging on the wall/ There's a saddle in a lonely stall / You ask me why my tear drops fall / It's that bridle hanging on the wall / And that pony for my guide I used to ride down the trail watching the moon beam low-ow —' (*The others stifling their laughter at him*)

MICHAEL ⎱ I need a drop more water for this one.

JUNIOR ⎰ One voice!

MICHAEL *joins* ANNE *at the bar.*

LIAM 'And the pony for my guide I used to ride down the trail / he's gone where the good ponies go-oh / There's a bridle hanging on the wall . . . . (*etc*)'

JUNIOR Lovely hurlin', cowboy!

PEGGY Smashin', Liam!

LIAM I must mosey to the john again, fellas.

TOM Hey!

LIAM Watch that latchyco, Anne!

TOM Hey! (*Calling after* LIAM, *stopping him*)

LIAM 'You ask me why my tear drops fall — '

TOM And *your* sisters or young brother will have the farm.

LIAM Sure, fella. (*Moving again*)

TOM Hey! (*Stopping him*) This eejit, this bollocks, with his auctioneering and tax-collecting and travel-agenting and property dealing and general greedy unprincipled poncing, and Sunday night dancing — Mr. successful-swinging-Ireland-In-The-Seventies! — and he's still — Jesus! — still — Jesus! — watching the few acres of bog at home, still — Jesus! — caught up in the few acres of bog around the house at home.

LIAM What — what would you say, fella, if I said it was mine already?

TOM I'd say, fella, that you're a liar.

LIAM Well, it is mine.

TOM As the bishop said to the actress.

LIAM By deed — By deed! — The deeds are signed over to me.

PEGGY But why suddenly all this talk tonight?

LIAM And my young brother is studying to be a doctor.

TOM Weren't you studying to be a doctor?

LIAM Oh, d'yeh hear him now?

TOM And quietly, it was a fortuitous outcome for the sick and the ailing that you never made it.

LIAM D'yeh hear him now — Tro'sky!

TOM And even if the young brother proves less thick than you, haven't the two spinster sisters a claim on the place?

LIAM By deed.

PEGGY But why —

TOM No — No deed. Because your attempts, and the details of your attempts, and the details of the failure of your attempts to upset them and evict them off the nine-and-a-half acre O'Brady estate are widely discussed and reported upon, in this town.

LIAM   I'm setting up my sisters in an antique shop.

JUNIOR   (*Quietly*) That's the place for them.

TOM   And quietly, and with little or no respect, I don't think either of them, in their advanced post-state of nubility, has much prospects of the bed.

LIAM   Oh d'yeh hear — I take exception to that remark.

TOM   Take what you like. Give us a drop of water here too for this one, Anne. So, the next time you see someone driving around in a Merc just think of him.

ANNE *arrives to add water to* TOM's *drink.*

LIAM   Why don't you get married?

TOM   Why don't yeh yourself? (*To* ANNE) That's fine (*He is rooting in his pockets again for further coins to pay for the last round*)

LIAM   Afraid of his Mammy and Daddy. And, d'ye know, he has to hand over his paypacket to his Mammy intact, every week, into her hand.

TOM   I get paid by cheque, Liam — monthly. (*To* ANNE) Just a sec.

ANNE   It's paid for —

TOM   Just a sec —

LIAM   Then cheque, countersigned, it has to be handed over to Mammy.

PEGGY   Aa, change the subject, lads.

ANNE   Junie paid for it.

JUNIOR   Sure poor auld Liam couldn't go bringing a woman into a house where there's three of them already —

PEGGY   (*Offering* TOM *two pounds*) Here, love —

TOM   (*To* ANNE) What?

JUNIOR   Jasus, they'd ate each other.

TOM   (*To* LIAM) You are the worst of the worst type of a ponce of a modern fuckin' gombeen man, that's all that's to be said about it.

ANNE   It's paid for, Tom.

LIAM   There's an answer for that one too.

TOM   Yes, Liam.

JUNIOR It's paid for, it's okay —
LIAM *(Only just containing his drunken fury)* My birthright!
TOM *(To* JUNIOR*)* What?
PEGGY Here, loveen —
TOM *(To* PEGGY*)* What?
LIAM That's no argument!
TOM *(To* LIAM*)* What?
JUNIOR It's okay, it's paid for —
TOM What?
LIAM The eldest son, fella!
TOM *(To* LIAM*)* What are you talking about? *(To* ANNE*)* And who asked anyone to pay for it! *(To himself)* Tck! — Look — Jesus — *(To* LIAM*)* Look, don't talk to me about argument — Look — lookit, don't talk to me at all! *(To* PEGGY*)* Will-you-put-that *(money)* — away! *(To* LIAM*)* You're only a fuckin' bunch of keys! *(To* ANNE*)* Bring us another round!

> ANNE *returns to bar.*

PEGGY Why don't you drive up and bring Gloria down. Do, Junie.
JUNIOR Oh-oh.
PEGGY Aa go on, good lad, do, do.
JUNIOR Won't I be seeing her later!
LIAM *(Quietly)* I'll squeeze your head for you some night, Ryan.
TOM Good man. My round is coming, is it Anne?
LIAM Cause I hate ye all — and all belongin' to ye!

> *He sweeps up his newspaper, then wrong-foots himself in his indecision as to whether to leave or not, remembers he has a stake in the place and exits to the Gents.*

JUNIOR Once you go once you're knackered for the evening.

> MICHAEL *laughing with* JUNIOR, *then* TOM *starts to chuckle and he joins* MICHAEL *and* ANNE *at the counter.*

ANNE But he's a lovely dancer though.

TOM, MICHAEL, JUNIOR *laughing again.* ANNE *joining in.*

TOM Now: the new generation: 'you ask me why my tear drops fall, it's that pony hangin' on the wall'.

Excepting PEGGY *they are laughing again. And* JUNIOR *is now rising to go to the Gents.*

JUNIOR Jasus, Jasus — (*To* PEGGY) Excuse me, the call of the wild, the enemy within — you have a great pair of kidneys, Ridge! — shake hands with the devil, wuw!

And he has exited to the Gents. PEGGY *now continues self-consciously isolated at the table, her back to the others. And they have all but forgotten her. Tom's mood is now pacificatory.*

ANNE What part are you in, Michael?
MICHAEL Well, I'm not working, obviously, at the moment, but —
TOM What part of America she's asking, eejit.

MICHAEL *looks at him:* TOM *gestures/shrugs that no malice is intended.*

MICHAEL New York.
ANNE What's it like?
MICHAEL Well, it's not too bad at all. Were you ever in the States?
ANNE No, but I was in London last summer. Two of us went over and we stayed with some friends of Daddy's.
MICHAEL Did you? Did he arrange it for you?
ANNE Yes.
PEGGY (*Isolated*) Indeed I was there myself for a few months once.

Nobody is listening to her.

ANNE We went to a place — I said I was eighteen — and got a job in an ice-cream factory.
PEGGY I was putting the tops on polish tins.

63

ANNE *has set up the other round.*

TOM Make that a double for your man (*Michael*) and mine the same and tell your mother to put it on the slate.

MICHAEL I'll get it.

TOM Don't be so extravagant with your mother's money. (*Then gestures/shrugs again to Michael's 'reaction: no malice intended; and showing Michael the few coins in his hand*) Look at the way I am myself.

ANNE And will I make the others doubles?

TOM Are yeh coddin' me!

MICHAEL What would you say to a stroll down to Woodlawn tomorrow, Anne?

She nods. This forthright reply, the immediate success of his proposition surprises and stops him for a moment.

ANNE Fine.

MICHAEL What?

ANNE That'd be lovely . . . What time? (*He gestures: what time would suit her*) Four.

MICHAEL (*Nods*) . . . Where shall I . . . ? (*meet you*)

ANNE The Bridge.

MICHAEL Ah! The Bridge.

LIAM *comes in and stands away from them, aloof, sulking.* MICHAEL *has started singing/performing — perhaps Rex Harrison/James Cagney style — for* ANNE.

MICHAEL 'At seventeen he falls in love quite madly with eyes of tender blue.'

TOM (*To* LIAM) There's a drink there for you, bollocks.

MICHAEL 'At twenty-four, he gets it rather badly with eyes of a different hue.'

TOM (*To* ANNE) Give him (*Liam*) that.

MICHAEL 'At thirty-five, you'll find him flirting sadly with two, or three, or more.'

TOM (*Edging him further away from the others*) Come over

64

MICHAEL   here a minute.

MICHAEL   'When he fancies he is past love' —

TOM   This is nonsense, this caper all evening.

MICHAEL   'It is then he meets his last love — '

TOM   Don't mind that. Hmm?

MICHAEL   Well, what's up with you?

TOM   Nothing. What's up with you?

MICHAEL   Not a thing.

TOM   Well then. Good luck!

MICHAEL   Good luck!

Short pause. Both looking down; can't think of anything to say.

MICHAEL   'And he loves her as he's never loved before.'

TOM   I can't help it . . . I can't feel anything about anything anymore.

MICHAEL   I know.

TOM   What?

MICHAEL   I know what you mean.

TOM   You're the only friend I have . . . Wha'?

MICHAEL   Mutual.

TOM   Say something.

MICHAEL   (*Quietly*) . . . Yahoo?

TOM   Did JJ admire me?

MICHAEL   Yeh.

TOM   (*To himself*) But what good is that? I don't think he understood my (*sighs*) situation. Isn't that what people want? What? A true and honest account of the situation first. What? A bit of clarity and sanity. Definition. Facts. Wha'? . . . Did he admire me?

MICHAEL   Yeh.

TOM   More than the others, you said.

MICHAEL   Bigger expectations (*shrugs*) — I suppose.

TOM   What? . . . Will I tell you something? What? Will I? Will I tell you something confidential? What? Will I? I never lost an argument in my life. What? What d'yeh think of that? What? Isn't that something? . . . But you're doing well.

MICHAEL   No.

TOM   No! You are!

MICHAEL   Setting myself on fire.

TOM   You're doing well, you're doing well, someone has to be doing well, and we're all delighted, we are, we are, we really are . . . The only friend I have, bollocks, with your cigarette holder in your top pocket. (MICHAEL'S *hand guiltily to his top pocket.* TOM *intensly, drunkenly*) Why didn't yeh use it, why didn't yeh use it?

MICHAEL   Just one of them filter things.

TOM   But why didn't yeh use it? D'yeh see what I mean? . . . (*Genuinely pained*) I try. I can't help it.

PEGGY   (*Rising, approaching, smiling bravely*) What are the men talking about? I know well: the women are always left out of the juicy things.

TOM   (*Frowning to himself*) What?

PEGGY   Cheers!

TOM   What?

MICHAEL   Cheers, Peggy.

PEGGY   Do you ever meet anyone from round here over there, Michael?

MICHAEL   Oh, I met Casey.

PEGGY   Aa did yeh. Joe? D'yeh hear that, love. How's he getting on?

MICHAEL   Fine. Getting the dollars regular every week, hot and cold water in his room, and paying no income tax.

PEGGY   Indeed we heard the opposite.

TOM   Hold it a second, Peg —

PEGGY   Someone who saw him over there —

TOM   A minute, Peg —

PEGGY   No shirt, an old pullover, no heels to his shoes —

TOM   Why do you always reduce everything!

PEGGY   . . . Well it was you told me.

Off, the town clock ringing eleven.

MICHAEL   One for the road, Anne. (*Extricating himself from* TOM *and* PEGGY)

JUNIOR   (*Off, and entering*) 'Oi, oi, oi, Delilah, phy, phy, phy, Delilah — ' (*He surveys the room*) Jasus, I was at better parties in the Mercy Convent!

MICHAEL (*Kicking cigarette holder across the room*) I don't give a damn. A walk in the woods, a breath of fresh air, right Anne?

She smiles, nods.

JUNIOR Into the net, Seaneen!
LIAM (*Glowering; a warning*) Watch it. (*The cigarette holder flying past him*)
JUNIOR Keep the faith, cowboy! I'll sing a hymn to Mary, he says, the mother of them all!
MICHAEL Let me ride the waves or let me drown! Am I fat, am I foolish!
LIAM (ANNE *has brought a drink to him*) Nothing for me. (*He spills the drink* TOM *bought him and the one that has just arrived on the floor and continues brooding*)
JUNIOR (*Singing*) 'The virgin of all virgins of God's own dearly son!'
MICHAEL 'Of David's royal blood'.
JUNIOR 'Of David's royal blood'.
MICHAEL Nice and quiet, Junie. (*They sing together,* ANNE *singing with them*) 'Oh teach me Holy Mary a loving song to frame / When wicked men blaspheme Thee / I'll love and bless Thy name / Oh Lily of the Valley . . .' (*Etc., until it is stopped by Tom's attack on Peggy*)
TOM (*Through the above, muttering*) Ugliness, ugliness, ugliness. (*He becomes aware of* PEGGY) What are you looking at?

PEGGY *has been casting hopeful glances at him. She does not reply.* MICHAEL, JUNIOR *and* ANNE *continue softly — under the following:*

TOM (*To* PEGGY) Do even *you* admire me? My feverish social writings.
PEGGY It's late, love.
TOM My generous warm humour.
PEGGY I'd like to go home, love.
TOM What?
PEGGY I don't feel well, love.

TOM What? Well, go! Who's stopping yeh? My God you walk up and down from your own house twenty times a day with your short little legs! No one will molest you! We're all mice!

She hurries from the room, stops in the front doorway, can't leave, her life invested in TOM — *and hangs in the doorway crying. Off, the church clock ringing eleven.*

MICHAEL (*About to follow* PEGGY) Ah Jesus, sham.

TOM (*Stops him with his voice*) Hey! (*Then*) Ugliness, ugliness, ugliness!

ANNE She's not feeling well.

TOM (*Stopping* MICHAEL *again with his voice and warning him not to interfere*) Hey! Gentlemen! Jim! My extravagant adventurous spirit. And the warm wild humour of Liam over there. And all those men of prudence and endeavour who would sell the little we have left of charm, character, kindness and madness to any old bidder with a pound, a dollar, a mark or a yen. And all those honest and honourable men who campaign for the right party and collect taxes on the chapel road. And all those honest and honourable men who are cutting down the trees for making — Easter-egg boxes!

MICHAEL That's more like it!

TOM Is it? (*Stopping* MICHAEL *again from going out to* PEGGY) Hey!

JUNIOR (*Quietly to* MICHAEL) Leave it so.

MICHAEL Let us remember that civility is not a sign of weakness —

TOM (*Mimics Kennedy*) 'And that sincerity is always subject to proof.' You all love speeches, rhetoric, crap, speeches. Right! 'I know you all, and will a while uphold the unyoked humour of your idleness.' I was always a better actor than you, better at everything than anyone round here. 'Yet herein will I imitate the sun who doth permit the base 'contagious clouds to smother up his beauty from the world'!

MICHAEL 'But when he please again to be himself — '

TOM *That!* '*That* when he please again to be himself, being wanted, he may be more wondered at, by breaking through the foul and ugly mists of vapour that seem to strangle him', tangle him, bangle him . . . .

VOICE) (*Off*) Goodnight to ye now.

JUNIOR | Good luck, Johnny!

ANNE (Good night, Johnny!

MICHAEL) Deoch an dorais, Tom, come on.

TOM (*Quietly: going — now docilely — to bar with* MICHAEL)
'And when this loose behaviour I throw off, by how much better than my word I am, my reformation glittering o'er my faults shall show more goodly and attract more eyes than this which hath no foil to set it off.'

> *Through this last section,* PEGGY *is in the doorway — she has had her head to the wall, crying — now listening, hoping someone will come out to her. She starts to sing   at first tentatively, like someone making noises to attract attention to herself. Then progressively, going into herself, singing essentially for herself: quietly, looking out at the night, her back to us, the sound representing her loneliness, the gentle desperation of her situation, and the memory of a decade ago. Her song creates a stillness over them all.*

PEGGY 'All in the April evening, April airs were abroad / The sheep with their little lambs passed me by on the road / The sheep with their little lambs passed me by on the road / All in the April evening I thought on the lamb of God.'

> *At the conclusion of the song,* MISSUS *coming down the stairs.* PEGGY *instinctively moving out of the doorway to stand outside the pub.*

TOM (*Quietly*) 'I'll so offend to make offence a skill, redeeming time when men think least I will.'

> MISSUS *comes in to collect a broom.*

MISSUS Come on now, boys, it's gone the time.

TOM One for the road, Missus.

MISSUS (*Returning to the public bar*) And Johnny Quinn is half-way home the back way to his bed by now.

JUNIOR Well, that's it.

LIAM Well, that's not it! (*He rattles a chair: his statement of challenge to fight*) I can quote more Shakespeare than any man here! (*He glances at each of them in turn, culminating with Tom*)

MISSUS (*Off*) Drink up now, boys!

LIAM 'And still they marvelled and the wonder grew, that one *big* head could carry all he knew.'

TOM (*Eyes closed*) Shakespeare?

LIAM No. Goldsmith.

JUNIOR Well said, boy.

LIAM *The Deserted Village*, fella.

MISSUS (*Off*) Finish up now, boys!

LIAM Ryan! The village schoolmaster . . . The f-f-f- . . . The f-f-f . . . Ryan! (LIAM *breathing heavily through his nose, jaws set, fists clenched.* TOM, *still with eyes closed, arms limply at his sides, turns to* LIAM, *nods, prepared to be hit (perhaps wanting to be hit)* The Village Schoolmaster. (TOM, *eyes closed, nods again.* LIAM, *unsure as to whether or not he is being mocked, glancing at the others . . . then suddenly grabs Tom's hand and shakes it.*

MISSUS (*Coming in with broom which she gives to* ANNE) And the guards are on the prowl these nights.

TOM (*To* LIAM) So are we quits?

LIAM Okay, fella.

TOM (*Glancing at* MICHAEL) But we're not quite though.

PEGGY *comes in timidly, gets her coat, hopeful glances at Tom.*

MICHAEL We're going to start again with a constant flow of good ideas. 'Let the word go forth . . .'

TOM (*By way of apology to* PEGGY) Just . . . just a bit of Shakespeare.

MICHAEL 'From this time and place, to friend and foe alike, that the torch has been passed to a new generation.'

MISSUS Come on now boys, come on.

JUNIOR Well I must be getting home anyway to Gloria — Oosh!

MICHAEL 'Let every nation know, whether it wishes us good or ill, that we shall pay any price, bear any burden, endure any hardship, to ensure the success and the survival of liberty.'

MISSUS (*To* LIAM) Call again during the week, Liam — why wouldn't yeh — and have a nice bite of tea with us. And thanks, the good boy, Liam. Drink up now, boys, and haven't ye all night tomorrow night, and thanks, thank ye all now. Yas. And safe home. D'ye know now.

She has switched off the lights in the lounge — (the spill of light from the hallway and from the public bar now lights the lounge) — and she is on her way along the hallway, upstairs, counting the money from her cardigan pockets. ANNE *is about to exit with the broom and some dirty glasses to public bar.*

MICHAEL Goodnight, princess, till it be morrow.

ANNE Goodnight. (*And exits to public bar*)

They are pulling on their coats, etc. in silence. JUNIOR *scrutinising the table for any drink that might have been left unfinished.*

MICHAEL But it wasn't a bad night.

JUNIOR It wasn't a bad auld night alright. (*And eager for further confirmation of this*) Wha'?

LIAM (*Muttering*) I wouldn't advise anyone to go messing with my plans.

MICHAEL And I'll be wheeling Annette tomorrow.

TOM Good man.

PEGGY Oh come on, loveen, I'm perished.

LIAM (*Muttering*) I know a thing or two about you, Ridge.

PEGGY What's he muttering about?

MICHAEL (*Singing quietly*) 'Sure no letter I'll be mailin'' —

LIAM It's not right.

MICHAEL 'For soon will I be sailin'' —

PEGGY Brrah, come on, loveen.

TOM (*Sudden thought*) Wait a minute.

MICHAEL 'And I'll bless the ship that takes me — '

TOM It's not right alright —

MICHAEL 'To my dear auld Erin's shore — '

TOM Michael. Anne.

MICHAEL } 'There I'll settle down forever — '

TOM } Serious — Michael — Don't start messin'.

MICHAEL } What?

LIAM Don't start messin' fella. Invested time and money. My — our territory. Right, Tom? Junie?

MICHAEL (*Laughs*) 'There's a pretty spot in Ireland — '

TOM Michael. Are you listening?

MICHAEL It's not a jiggy-jig job. JJ's daughter. A walk in the wood, a breath of fresh air. (*He looks at their serious faces*) What? You know it's nothing else.

TOM We don't.

LIAM We don't, fella. A word to Mrs. Kilkelly — or to Anne herself.

TOM So cop on.

MICHAEL Who?

TOM You.

LIAM You, fella. Don't infringe.

MICHAEL *looks incredulously at* TOM.

TOM (*Shrugs/blandly*) Liam's territory. Right Liam, you nearly have it sold, right? Good. Even if they don't know it. Better for Missus, Anne. Better for — Put a bomb under it if you like. Better for everyone. Reality. So that's okay. And we'll fix you up with the gammy one tomorrow. Josephine. Right, Junie?

JUNIOR (*Has enough of them*) I'm off. Jasus, I only meant to have the two pints. (*To* MICHAEL) D'yeh want a lift? (*To* TOM *and* PEGGY) D'ye want a lift? Okay, see ye.

He goes off, puffing a tuneless whistle and a few moments later we hear him drive away.

PEGGY Oh come on, loveen, your mother will have your life.

TOM Don't be silly!

LIAM So that's okay then, Tom?

TOM (*Quietly but firmly*) Yeh.

LIAM Okay, fellas. God bless.

He exits.

TOM . . . I hope he remembers he has no clutch in his car or
he'll be all night looking for it. (LIAM'S *car starting up and
driving away*) . . . Come on, we'll walk you home.

MICHAEL I'm dead sober. And I'm certainly not as confused as I
was.

TOM (*Pacificatory*) Ary! You're only an eejit, Ridge. (MICHAEL
nods)

PEGGY Y'are. (MICHAEL *nods*)

TOM (*Mock gruffness*) Y'are!

MICHAEL But I know what I came home for.

TOM Come on, we'll walk yeh down.

MICHAEL No, I'm — okay.

TOM Give us a shout tomorrow.

PEGGY Night-night, Michael.

TOM We didn't get a chance to have a right talk.

PEGGY God bless, take care.

TOM Good luck, sham.

MICHAEL Good luck.

TOM *and* PEGGY *exit.*

TOM (*Off*) Give us a shout tomorrow!

PEGGY (*Off*) 'Bye-'bye, Michael!

TOM (*Off*) Will yeh?

PEGGY (*Off*) 'Bye-'bye, Michael!

TOM (*Off*) Will yeh?

PEGGY (*Off*) 'Bye-'bye!

*Michael continues standing there. He looks up and
around the room. He finishes his drink and is about to
leave.*

MISSUS (*Off*) Leave the light on in the hall, Annette, in case.

The light is switched off in the public bar and ANNE
enters and discovers MICHAEL. *Her simple grave*

73

expression.

MICHAEL (*Whispers*) I have to go in the morning.
ANNE (*Silently*) What?
MICHAEL Have to go in the morning. (*He smiles, shrugs*) They've probably cut down the rest of the wood by now, anyway.
ANNE There's still the stream.
MICHAEL Yeh. But I have to go. Tell JJ I'm sorry I didn't see him. Tell him . . . (*He wants to add something but cannot find the words yet*) . . . Tell him I love him.

She nods, she smiles, she knows. He waits for another moment to admire her, then he walks off. ANNE *continues in the window as at the beginning of the play, smiling her gentle hope out at the night.*